# Compassion Revolution

## Start Now
## Use What You Have
## Keep Going

## Mary Freer

# Praise for Mary Freer's *Compassion Revolution*

Every single time I meet Mary I feel better about myself, my life and the world around me. I don't know how that happens, but if this book comes anywhere close to explaining it, you must buy it for everyone you know. Straight away.
*Ross Fisher, Consultant Paediatric Surgeon,*
*Sheffield Children's Hospital*

Mary's work is a magical light shining in our world. Her words are a generous warm embrace filled with wisdom, comfort and compassion. She's someone for both a time of need as well as joy.
*Michael Lewarne, Architect and Founder: unmeasured*

Mary Freer is a marvel.

The way she brings people together to imagine new futures for healthcare is filled with energy, curiosity and joy. Mary leads from a deep understanding of healthcare as a human system. As a consumer and as a researcher, I value Mary's commitment to good evidence and to achieving change that puts people first. What you learn from Mary's events will keep you thinking for a long time.
*Assoc. Professor Kate Bowles, University of Wollongong*

Mary Freer brings a fresh perspective to the role of compassion in our lives.

This has really resonated with me personally and many of our staff at Ambulance Victoria who have attended her workshops and conferences. She has an innate ability to bring those from different backgrounds together for a common purpose.
*Professor Tony Walker, Chief Executive Officer, Ambulance Victoria*

Mary Freer's insight into Compassion is like a hot cup of tea on a cold, grey and wet afternoon. Nurturing, warming and best savoured. Her ideas have a knack for showing up right when you need them most and gently guide you to be your most compassionate, brave self.
*Peter Shepherd, Founder and Director, Human Periscope*

Compassion is often looked upon as intangible; something that's nice to have, but hard to pin down. Mary Freer's work speaks directly to the tangible side of compassion: its personal, social and even financial impact, and the ways you can bring it into your own world.
*Kirsty Stark, Producer, Epic Films*

Mary is a visionary.

She is a transformative and inclusive leader who inspires and amplifies the leadership and learning of others through her work, events and training.
*Jane Sloane, Director, Women's Empowerment Program,*
*The Asia Foundation*

Mary is the real deal.

She transformed the way I conceptualise compassion: a muscular strength best tended to with attention and delight. Anything Mary leads is a "YES PLEASE!" for me.
*Shannon Weber, Author of 'Show Up Hard: A Roadmap for*
*Helpers in Crisis'*

Mary has brought a breath of fresh air to our medical community.

She has reinvigorated our energy and reminded us to focus on compassion – not only for our patients, but also for ourselves.
*Tessa Davis, Consultant in Paediatric Emergency Medicine, Royal London Hospital and Senior Lecturer, Queen Mary University of London*

Mary has been our fairy godmother, sprinkling compassion over everything she does.

Whether she is conducting one-on-one interviews with Hollywood stars, facilitating small group workshops or hosting large events, she makes sure the audience knows that it is never about her, but about us, and how we can all be compassionate.
*Andrew Tagg, Emergency Medicine Consultant and Co-founder of Don't Forget The Bubbles*

I am who I am, doing what I came to do.
Audre Lorde

For Audrey. My joy in you is immeasurable.

# Welcome Note

Welcome dear Compassion Revolutionary!

I've been waiting for you. I have thought about you every day since I started writing this book. I have imagined you rising early in the middle of winter as you prepared for another long day at work or another night on shift. The hours are long for you and when you drive home early in the morning, I'm anxious you will fall asleep at the wheel. If I could, I would hail a cab for you and hold the umbrella while you clamber in.

I sometimes see you eating ice-cream by the light of the fridge door or waiting by the vending machine for something in a red wrapper to drop into your hand. Sometimes at night you lie awake running through a list of all the possible ways the day might have turned out if only this or that had happened. Some days you sit very still and look into the milky eyes of that 97-year-old woman who wants the pain to end and other days you manage scenarios that leave you breathless and exhausted. You've juggled demands to make things work better for someone else. You have audacious dreams and endless emails. There is a paper trail that stretches out into a future that you want to carve into something wonderful.

At night when you arrive home after a long day of back-to-back meetings and zoom calls, you stand at the foot of your child's bed and inhale the sweet smell of sleep and feel the shudder of time passing too quickly.

I hope you know that you are deeply loved and appreciated by many and that even now as you read this sentence, someone is thinking about you and wondering when they will see your face again. Even as the years pass and you have long forgotten this moment, someone, somewhere will be thinking of you and remembering the day your words made all the difference. It's delightful to see you at your playful best. In those moments I imagine you throwing your head back and laughing from your belly. Do more of that, it cheers the entire world up.

I know how much you care for others and the skill and effort you exert to make this world a safer place. Some days you judge yourself too harshly and then armour yourself up. But the thing I love the most about you is that you never give up. I'll be honest; there have been times that I have worried about how tired you have become and I hoped that you were being fully supported and that your needs were the priority for someone who could do something to make life easier. More than anything else, I have come to understand your courage and your tender heartedness, your thoughtfulness and your generosity.

If I could, I would write you a note and slip it to you as we passed each other in the corridor or while we waited in line for our coffee. On the ride home you would open it and see my scribble. *Your heart is a shining star.*

This is the place where we are meant to be.

Let's keep going,

Mary

Sometimes we need to let ourselves be held by a little prayer of encouragement from others. For the days when it feels too big this is for you.

First published in 2021 by Mary Freer



A catalogue entry for this book is available from the National Library of Australia.

ISBN: 978-1-922553-80-5

Project management and text design by Publish Central

**Disclaimer**

The material in this publication is of the nature of general comment only, and does not represent professional advice. It is not intended to provide specific guidance for particular circumstances and it should not be relied on as the basis for any decision to take action or not take action on any matter which it covers. Readers should obtain professional advice where appropriate, before making any such decision. To the maximum extent permitted by law, the author and publisher disclaim all responsibility and liability to any person, arising directly or indirectly from any person taking or not taking action based on the information in this publication.

# Contents

# Introduction

For thirty years, I have worked somewhere in the healthcare ecosystem. My career started as a newly minted social worker trying to figure out the child protection system. I packed up households full of belongings into green garbage bags while the police stood guard so we could move women and their children out of violence and into a shelter. I watched small children hold oversized crayons and draw their stories of abuse and pain and looming danger. I tried to make a plan for safety and hold space for things I was not prepared to hear. Night after night, I would come home from work, sit on my back step and feel the sickness rise into my throat. I would naively think that there was nothing to be done in a system that is broken.

I worked my way along a career trajectory as the director of a number of women's health services, a senior policy analyst, an academic, a strategic planning consultant and an executive in the C-suite. One morning I woke up and could hear another world calling. I walked straight into a beautiful crazy idea to build a grassroots social action to encourage healthcare workers to make changes right where they were. During a three-year period, over 100,000 health and aged care workers made a promise on the

Change Day Australia website to do one thing to improve the system they worked in. Their ideas, innovations, dreams and actions were powerful.

On the back of this work, I was awarded a prestigious Westpac Foundation Social Change Fellowship. My aim was to cultivate my awareness of compassion in a more systematic and whole-hearted way and to discover more about the connection between compassion and high-quality, safe and cost-effective healthcare.

On the long flight home to Australia after months on a study tour, my mind was buzzing. I started to write in my journal under the heading *So What Now?* By the time I had touched down in Melbourne some 22 hours later, I had a draft design for the first Compassion Lab, an experiential, evidence-based workshop, where people could train in compassion. Before long, doctors, nurses, hospital auxiliary staff, aged care workers, executives, CEOs, psychiatrists, not for profit leaders and entrepreneurs from London to Australia were joining the Compassion Labs.

The Compassion Labs[1] grew and soon I realised we had a Compassion Revolution on our hands. This book captures the ways I have come to understand and practise compassion in action.

Right now, more than anything else, we need compassion. Not a soft, fluffy idea of compassion but a compassion that is muscular. This book is about how we build that muscle. Across the world we need compassion as an axe to break down doors and bring us into a new epoch of justice. I learnt from activists like Grace Lee Boggs that we can be aware that we cannot continue to live and work in the same way but at the same time feel immobilised because we cannot imagine an alternative. Grace Lee Boggs held to the view that our way of being in the world and indeed the world we are 'being in' is not fixed or immutable.[2] But she also knew that we could not just turn our backs on the twisted shape of things. To imagine our way forward into something far more life-giving and sustainable, we need to own the way things are.

The COVID-19 pandemic has revealed (or as Jonathan Cohen put it, 'unearthed and exhumed from the places we chose to bury them'[3]) how ill-equipped our global health ecosystem is to address structural violence as a determinant of health. Across the world our health systems are underpinned by a history of slavery, genocide, stolen children, displaced communities, environmental racism and a predatory capitalism. This has resulted in health systems with structural, racial and ethnic inequities within Black, Indigenous and People of Colour (BIPOC) communities across the globe.[4] We have developed over many centuries a system of providing health that is centred on exclusionary colonialist patterns that centre on Euro-Western knowledge systems. These systems are not only Euro-Western centric but they have also been historically used as tools of power and violence against BIPOC, leading to a genuine mistrust of medicine and the health systems it operates within.[5]

What we must do as Compassion Revolutionaries is to create a new world that values and respects people in all their complexity, diversity and humanity. We must resist all invitations, even the most subtle, to marginalise and dismiss others and instead create new bolder ways of relating to each other at work and at home. These new ways of relating will seem small but they are not insignificant. Everything that we do to resist the pull of the healthcare system towards a care-less economy is something and it is something very powerful. Every time we diverge from the taken for granted way of being in the workforce and enact more compassion is an act of mighty resistance. Every time we pause to recognise our common humanity we are celebrating the miracle of being alive. Eugenio Montejo is one of my all-time favourite poets. As I write these words, I cannot help but remember his poem that celebrates the miracle of connection.

'The earth turned to bring us closer, it spun on itself and within us and finally joined us together in this dream.' You and me and the young man who is paid almost nothing to deliver the presents we send ourselves from Amazon and leave them neatly by our front door. We are all joined together.

This is what it means to be a revolutionary. This is what it means to be compassionate. This is what it means to bring our whole selves.

This revolution of compassion will not happen because of an overthrow. It will happen because of a transition. We are in that transition. But first we have to own the system, knowing that we created it and now it is broken and we must build something new in its place.

When we keep compassion at the very centre of our practice, we become more resilient to stress and immune to burnout and we find our work more inspiring. When our organisations practise a culture of compassion we see a reduction in employee exhaustion and sick leave. These organisations will have a higher level of positive emotion for their staff. Put simply: compassionate organisations care for their people. The economic and moral return on this investment is significant.

We know that compassion makes moral and economic sense but how do we practise it and maintain our joy and care for ourselves? I have designed a simple four-step process to help you understand how compassion works. In Chapter Two, you will discover SUMA and the art of Showing Up, Understanding, Moving Closer and Acting. With practice, these steps will become your default response in times of happiness and distress.

As you read this book, you will grow your compassion muscle. You will also find creative ways to bring compassion alive inside your place of work and in the world. This is what Compassion Revolutionaries do. Right?

At the end of each chapter, I will give you a little workout for your compassion muscle. This is my invitation to you to practise leaning right into compassion's gravitational pull. Most of my examples are from the sector I know best – healthcare – but I am writing this book for anyone who serves. I know that teachers, artists, architects, parents and hospitality workers and others will all benefit from a compassion muscle workout.

Let's start right now, use what we have and keep going.

# 1

# Compassion is not a special project

## Introduction

> *Compassion is not religious business, it is human business,*
> *it is not luxury, it is essential for our own peace and mental*
> *stability, it is essential for human survival.*
>
> *His Holiness the Dalai Lama*

Hands up if you want human survival?

Perhaps the most often repeated question I hear from medical administrators and funding bodies is this: Can you show me the evidence that cultivating compassion will have a positive impact on outcomes? The simplest answer to this question is this:

> *the effects of compassion are greater than the effects of aspirin*
> *in the prevention of heart attacks, and of statins in the five*
> *year risk of a cardiovascular event.*[1]

That's some big impact, right there.

I sometimes have this weird daydream that one day, in a not too distant dystopian future, a pharmaceutical company will try and sell us compassion. They will market the efficacy based on their double blind, randomised controlled trials. They will promise that if we dispense compassion in the workplace it will improve the culture, increase our staff retention, save us money and make us happier and healthier. We will pay a fortune for it. We will eagerly open wide our mouths and swallow the pill and so we should, because that is absolutely what compassion does.

There are hundreds of research studies, thousands of years of contemplative practices across religions and the fMRI[2] scans of hundreds of brains, some of them belonging to long-term meditators, all telling us the same thing: compassion is essential for human health, creativity, innovation and safety. It is now established that connection and belonging are fundamental to us as human beings and provides us with 50 per cent higher chances of survival over time.[3] Neuroscientific studies suggest that the most powerful activator of brain circuits associated with happiness is compassion or helping others.[4] Helping other people makes us happy.

All of the accumulated evidence demonstrates that compassion makes a huge difference. In this chapter, I will introduce you to some of the research and evidence on the powerful benefits of compassion, from economic savings to higher creativity and saved lives.

## Behaviour spreads like a virus

When I was in my forties, I worked in one of the most dysfunctional teams I have ever seen. The stress was on constant boil and the policy was 'blame and run'. During this time, I developed an inflammatory auto-immune condition so I approached the CEO about some changes to my hours. He said, without a moment's hesitation,

'If I'd known you were going to get sick, I never would have employed you.' Later that day in a moment of *l'esprit de l'escalier*, I heard myself respond, 'If I'd known you were going to make me so sick I never would have taken the job.' Staircase wit is always clever, but at the time I said nothing, my face flushed with fury and I felt hot tears well up in my eyes. Then I went home and wasted hours rehashing the conversation. This is what most people do. We toss and turn in bed at 3am replaying the same old mix tape.

## Incivility

Rudeness, bullying, blaming, snide remarks, criticism, exclusion, racism, homophobia, transphobia and so many other destructive practices have a measurable impact on our experience of work, the quality of our performance and the resilience of our mental and physical wellbeing. The impact of workplace behaviours have been studied and the evidence is powerful. When we are treated disrespectfully or rudely, we disengage from our work. It may not happen overnight but it will happen.

In a workforce study by Christine Porath that covered 18 separate industries in the United States, only 33 per cent of workers felt fully engaged in their work.[5] Fifty-one per cent were disengaged and 16 per cent were actively disengaged. Porath put forward a proposition that this mirrors what is happening in other countries, including Australia.

I have seen this play out over and over again in workplaces all over Australia. If you think your staff are reluctant to come up with solutions or are low on creativity and innovation, it might be time to check how psychologically and physically safe your workplace really is.

There are also both short- and long-term outcomes of witnessing incivility in the workplace. Incivility can be spread, like a virus, and contaminate even the bystanders' behaviour over time. I coach lots of not for profit CEOs and entrepreneurs and I see this holding back their progress over and over again. It doesn't matter if you build houses, design apps or fly planes. If you work in a rude and dismissive environment, you will not be operating at your most creative or innovative level. All functioning of the brain depends on your internal state. As we move from one internal state to another there will be a shift in the parts of the brain that are dominant. Bruce Perry in his co-authored book *What Happened To You?* has measured the way our brain moves from abstract to reactive thinking as we move from calm to fear.[6] Our available IQ goes from 120-100 when we are in a calm state to 90-70 when we are fearful and 80-60 when we experience terror.

Maybe you think that while all this is true, it's not like this where you work. A recent study covering seven Australian hospitals found that 'unprofessional behaviour' is highly prevalent among hospital workers, with 39 per cent of those surveyed reporting weekly or more frequent incivility, bullying, discrimination and harassment by co-workers.[7] These behaviours have a direct impact on patient safety, healthcare delivery and staff wellbeing. Maybe you work in the aviation industry where incivility, especially in multi-crew cockpits, is inherently dangerous. It demoralises the pilot affected, leads to a rapid breakdown in communication, leads to poor crew resource management and ultimately reduces effectiveness and safety margins. It also affects emotions, performance, motivation, attention span, reduces available brain processing power and leads to performance degradation.

## The impact of rudeness on clinical outcomes

Researchers Amir Erez and others set out to determine what patients experience when staff speak rudely to each other in a healthcare setting.[8] They found that dismissive and uncivil behaviour has a direct and negative impact on patient outcomes.

Professor Erez and his colleagues set up a simulated study where 24 NICU (Neonatal Intensive Care Unit) teams participated in a training simulation involving a preterm infant whose condition acutely deteriorated due to necrotising enterocolitis. Participants were told that a visiting expert on Team Reflexivity in Medicine would observe them. Teams were randomly assigned to either exposure to rudeness or control. The videotaped simulation sessions were evaluated by three independent judges (blinded to team exposure) who used structured questionnaires to assess team performance, information-sharing and help-seeking.

Participants were told that they were going to be observed via a webcam. The Control Teams heard a voice recording played at the beginning and the observer said, 'Thank you for letting me observe you and please commence when you're ready.' They commenced the simulation, diagnosing and treating the infant. About 10 minutes later, the observer interrupted them to say 'Please keep going. I'll continue to observe you.'

The Rudeness Teams heard the voice of the observer say, 'I'm new to your country but from what I've seen so far, I hope I don't get sick, because I really don't trust this healthcare system.' At 10 minutes, he interrupted them to say, 'None of you would get a job in my department.'

Erez analysed the results after these different interactions with the observer and what he found was predictable but frightening. Where staff were spoken to rudely by the observer, it accounted for about 56 per cent of the errors that they made. It wasn't that the other team always got everything right but the teams that were spoken to rudely had a much higher rate of error. There was poor team diagnostic and procedural performance that included incorrect diagnosis, incorrect medication requests and dosage, and poor team cohesiveness which impacted on communication when it was critically needed.

Reading that piece of research was the moment where I felt the shove between my shoulder blades. Up until then, I'd thought that when we were rude to each other and when we treated each other in a dismissive way, it was bad for staff wellbeing (and it is). But when I read Erez's research, I realised it is much bigger than that. This behaviour kills people. I realised that people could go into hospital, relying on healthcare workers to look after them and to make them well, and that they could die at the expense of this behaviour. We need to be careful how we speak to each other.

When I was a small child, I believed that all the words you ever speak live on forever, continually circling the globe in ever-increasing waves. I would imagine that certain words were attracted to another and would form large clusters together somewhere in the sky. Kind words would create a slipstream and harsh and degrading words were like thick tar that clogged everything up. Words were not biodegradable, they had shape and presence and they were felt by others. If we spoke harsh or cruel words they would form a type of environmental pollution and everyone would suffer. This story I created about words had a big impact on me and to this day I tend carefully to the words I speak.

If words do carry weight, what words might you choose to carry and change?

## Compassion makes economic sense

*Show me the money!*

*Rod Tidwell*

Everything that you want to see happen in your organisation has to make good financial sense. You may think that compassion is important but will you be able to afford it? When you invest in your culture and make your organisation the place that people want to work and to turn up to every day, then you will decrease staff turnover. One of the things that bleeds money out of the healthcare system is a heavy reliance on agency staff. Not only do we increase the rate of errors because we have people coming into hospitals who are not familiar with processes, protocols, where things are and who patients are, but they are far more expensive. Each staff member costs money to induct and they carry information and wisdom about your organisation. When they walk out the door, they take that with them.

A large percentage of people will not engage with their work if they don't feel that they belong in or are cared for by their organisation. This lack of engagement costs billions of dollars each year in lost productivity.

Errors at work always have a cost associated with them, even if it is just a sense of pride that people are making an unnecessary mistake. When we invest in teams that are willing to take risks within reasonable boundaries because they don't feel they're going to encounter blame and shame, they're more likely to support each other and to experiment to get the best outcome. In healthcare, errors cost lives and often result in teams not working smoothly, not being able to communicate well or arise out of poor behaviour which has an impact on our ability to work at our best. In any workplace, lack of respect and support leads to errors and lack of engagement. Put simply: your frontal cortex doesn't work well when you're under threat.

You may be working in an organisation or a system that has let you down so badly over such a long period of time that you wonder whether change is even possible. As Kenny Rogers said, 'You've got to know when to hold 'em, know when to fold 'em, Know when to walk away, know when to run.'

While I don't want you to be disheartened, and I firmly believe that change across the healthcare ecosystem and other specific industry ecosystems is happening, I also know that there are times when you will need to step back, take a break or move on to work that is more nourishing. You don't have to set yourself on fire to keep other people warm. Keep in mind that you matter, your health matters and your time matters. Take care of yourself so you can keep showing up.

## Compassion doesn't take a lot of time

You're busy at work and you've got a million things to do. If you work in a large hospital, you've got numerous patients needing discharge by 10am, there are ambulances ramped up outside of the Emergency Department, discharge summaries to complete, long queues of people waiting for a COVID test, and then there's electronic medical records. You're run off your feet. But if you invest a little bit of time now, you will save an enormous amount of time upstream.

Earlier this year I entered the operating theatre for a procedure to remove what turned out to be a benign mass. I was nervous and my diastolic blood pressure was rising. I let myself imagine the possibility that I might have cancer. My surgeon and anesthesiologist were both very caring and warm. I can recall the moment before I drifted off to sleep. The surgeon leaned in close to my face and held my hand. She whispered, 'Mary, I will be there the whole time, trust me. Have a great sleep.' I woke up and felt safe. My pain was managed well and my recovery was uneventful. The surgeon visited me in the recovery ward and assured me that all had gone well, and she phoned me a few days later to explain my results. The research tells us that when surgical patients are encouraged by their anesthesiologists (in my case the surgeon) during the immediate postoperative period, they heal faster and are discharged from hospital sooner because they require up to 50 per cent less pain relieving medication.[9] How rewarding to know that your patients are recovering quickly and are in far less pain.

Taking time to be with people is important. Often we think if we can fob people off because we're so busy then we'll save a bit of time, but all we're really doing is saying, 'I don't have time, so I'm going to get this done quickly and pass it along.' I guarantee that whatever their problem or need or distress is, someone's going to have to hear it. We're just making a decision that today it's not going to be us.

Emergency Departments are frequently visited by a handful of individuals experiencing housing injustice and drug-dependency. Our cities are full of human beings who are trying to stay alive in harsh circumstances; these people will often end up in Emergency Departments. Many Emergency Departments that I work with are caught between wanting to care and the organisational imperative to move people on. I've seen instructions in case notes – do not give a blanket or food. If they're not sick, keep them moving.

But people are heat-seeking missiles and they will continue to return until they feel that their needs are met. A Canadian RCT that was reported in *The Lancet* found that treating homeless patients with usual treatment plus extra compassion resulted in a 33 per cent decrease in the number of return visits to the ED in the following 30 days.[10] We think that if we are dismissive and we keep turning people away then they're probably not going to come back but it's counter-intuitive. It makes sense because when people leave the ED, they don't think, 'Oh, there's nothing wrong with me, that's why they sent me away.' Generally, they think, 'If I had only explained my situation more clearly, they would've understood how unwell I am.' Or maybe they feel so unwell because they're stressed, lonely, hungry and cold. If you take a moment to be compassionate it will save you time.

A palliative care physician told me recently that the bed manager at his hospital called to ask how quickly he could free up a bed that had been occupied by a patient who had died but was still warm. In that moment he was demoralised by the way a body can be reduced to a unit that blocks the availability of beds. In healthcare, we are whipped by metrics. The monitoring of hospital admissions, discharge and patient movement within the hospital is a tireless task that is scrutinised by governance committees and completely mystifying to patients and their families. But the care of patients isn't a high stakes Tetris game.

Kathy Torpie was a patient in an intensive care unit in New Zealand after a multi-trauma accident.[11] She went on to become a vocal advocate for compassionate care. In a recorded workshop Kathy talks about the 'one special nurse' who cared for her when she couldn't open her eyes, couldn't feed herself and couldn't move. This nurse would do exactly the same jobs as the other nurses – checking her IV line, washing her, changing her clothes, checking her charts – but while he was doing it, he always talked to her. He talked about everyday things. She recalls how these moments made her feel '… less than a broken body.' This one special nurse didn't spend more time than his work allowed, but he used the time that he had to make a connection.

Isn't this exactly why you decided to do the work you do? Didn't you start out wanting to be the one who connected to patients, students, customers, clients, people in need? When compassion is the thing that gets stripped away and all you're left with is the mechanics of healthcare or your organisation's structure, you will feel miserable. You want to connect with your patients, with your customers, with the people you serve. It won't take more time. It will take effort.

## Compassion makes us better people and increases our creativity

Compassion increases our creativity. Professor Christine Porath carried out an activity where she tested how creative people were after they had been spoken to by the 'grumpy professor'.[12] She had participants move through the university campus on their way to a creativity class, and half of them bumped into a professor who gave them a dressing down and told them they were wasting his time. When they turned up at their class on creativity, the people who had bumped into the grumpy professor were far less creative and when she asked them questions like, 'What are all the uses you can have for a brick?' they came up with fewer and less exciting or interesting ideas than the others. She was able to measure how creative people are when they encounter rudeness.

We're not as creative and we're also not as innovative. We talk a lot about wanting an innovative organisation and the ways to increase compassion and innovation are exactly the same. When people feel safe while taking risks within boundaries, they are far more innovative and creative, and there's more compassion at play. It also makes us feel better. When we see others behaving in a compassionate way, it releases oxytocin in our bodies and we start to feel happier.

Compassion is contagious. If you start to behave with care and compassion to people around you, other people witnessing that will also start to behave in that way. It's like a Mexican wave that you're spreading through your workplace. Take an opportunity to act with compassion and before you know it, other people are doing that as well.

Be mindful of your wake. We don't know what is happening in a room when we're not there, and often someone will give us feedback about how they missed us when we weren't at a meeting, 'Oh, I wish you'd been there. It would have been so much more creative.'

When we're in the room, we think that the positive vibe and the wonderful things that are happening are the responsibility of everybody else, but we bring energy into the room, too.

You've probably worked with people who, when you know they're going to be at a meeting, you think, 'Oh, god, how can I get out of it?' Then there are other people who, when you think they're going to be on the team, your first thought is, 'Oh, this is going to be good. We're going to achieve something.' Think about what you leave behind when you leave the room or the meeting. Do you leave people feeling better about themselves and better about the work? Do you leave them feeling more capable of reaching goals and sharing the load? Or do you leave them wondering how they're going to get anything done?

# Compassion muscle workout

## Being present

Over the next few days, practise being present with people. I don't mean just being in the room. One of the requirements for compassion is that we show up and be where we are, not be somewhere else. I want you to really be there when you're with people. If you're in, be all in. If you're with your staff, don't scroll on your phone. If you're with your partner, don't plan the morning round. If you're talking to a colleague, stay focused and try not to let your mind drift away to other pressing problems. You're going to notice exactly what the research tells us – most of the time we're not even thinking about the thing we're doing. That's how we manage to drive home, get into the driveway and say to ourselves, 'How the hell did I get here?' We're human beings and our minds are adrift, so we're going to practise being right where we are for a few moments every day.

## The energy you leave

Sometimes we forget to check in and see the impact we're having on others. Make a commitment and write yourself a note right now which says, 'What energy do I want to leave behind?' Start to check in. You could also include it on the agenda of a meeting. Ask people at the end of meetings, like I often do, 'What's one word to describe how we're feeling now?' Check in and collect data on how people are feeling. How confident are people feeling? What else do they need from you? More importantly, how can you help? Check in with yourself: How am I feeling in my body? We carry around with ourselves a body that is collecting and storing information constantly. To all the readers who keep asking me for evidence – join me and check in with your body. What is it telling you?

## Questions to consider

How might you present the evidence about compassion to your team or organisation? Will you gather some facts and stories from this book and elsewhere and create a short presentation? Remember that stories are equally important and will have greater appeal to your audience. Especially if the stories are meaningful to you.

How will you capture the changes you see as you build up your compassion muscle? Will you keep notes in a journal? Maybe you will capture your team's one word feeling answers in your regular meetings.

What would a reading circle be like where you work? This could be as simple as finding 4-12 people who will commit to reading this book with you and discussing the ways you might collectively make some changes where you work. I suggest you catch up each fortnight for one hour and learn together.

## Conclusion

Anyone who works in our healthcare system knows that at the end of a straight run of night shifts, when your dehydrated body seems to be caught in an extended jet lag, and your boss has slammed the phone down on you: 100 yoga mats and a litre of ginger tea won't solve this mess. The same goes for a parent of a child with autism, a teacher swamped with parent interviews and reports to write or a psychologist in the middle of a pandemic. When your organisation is heading for a monumental overspend and the ambulances are ramping up outside the Emergency Department because the system cannot complete timely discharges and has no capacity to receive any further patients until the bottleneck has eased, you need clarity, emotional tenacity and the will to make a difference. That is compassion in action.

In this chapter, you have learned that compassion has a real payoff. It's worthwhile investing in compassion and developing your compassion muscle. It's not soft or fluffy. Compassion is mainstream. The days of it being a nice add-on are over. It's now vitally important for getting business done. You can change the way you do things at work and see a direct benefit. You now have an argument for the case of investing in compassion. You are a Compassion Revolutionary and you have my full permission to agitate for more compassion where you work.

In the next chapter, we're going to look at compassion in much more depth. I've given you the science and the evidence, but how do we practise it? What does it mean? Is compassion the same as kindness? Is it the same as empathy? It's far more than both of those and we're going to discuss that in Chapter Two.

# 2

# What is compassion?

## Introduction

*We are each made for goodness, love and compassion. Our lives are transformed as much as the world is when we live with these truths.*

*Desmond Tutu*

Humans have this incredible capacity for violence and cruelty, but we also have a well-documented and clear biological, cultural, neurobiological, endocrinological capacity for care and compassion. It always amazes me how much humans can care. When we hold a tiny baby we have little trouble believing in the idea that they will naturally develop their own capacity for compassion. They have come into this world ready to love and be loved in return. If they are fortunate enough to be born into a compassionate community or family, they will develop finely tuned compassion over time as they grow. This occurs in the same way that children are born with the capacity to use language. But if they are deprived of language and they are not raised in a linguistic community, they will not learn to use language. We need a linguistic community to learn how to use and develop our language skills and we need a compassionate community to learn how to develop compassion.

In this chapter, I'm setting out to illuminate your understanding of compassion. To do this I need you to put all those ideas you might have about compassion being soft and fluffy to one side. Pack them up and put them away. Those ideas will only hold you back. The kind of compassion I'm interested in is muscular. It is brave. Compassion is often fearless and forthright. At times it can be best described as Radical Compassion: a compassion that is fueled by the urgent call for social justice. Just when you think compassion is exactly what you need to answer the clarion call for a system change, you get a glimpse of compassion at the bedside. At that moment, compassion is quiet and still and simply holding space for what is unfolding. At other times compassion is the silence that brings just enough tension to make a way through a deadlock. This compassion blows whistles and stops the line, she puts out fires and lights others. But above all else, compassion always sees the distress and suffering that we and others are experiencing and finds a way to alleviate that distress. She is a tactician, a balm, a life raft, a fortress and a way through. She is the brave space but not always the safe space. When she holds your gaze, you know you have been seen and accepted.

I want you to understand what compassion is and what it isn't.

Compassion is not the same as kindness. I'm all for kindness, I think the world needs more meticulously premeditated and also completely random acts of kindness. Often when I tell people that compassion isn't the same as kindness, they mistakenly think I don't value kindness. I think kindness is stitched into the lining of compassion but it is not the coat. To make it more confusing the terms kindness and compassion are often used interchangeably.

We can practise kindness to each other at work by making an extra cup of tea or greeting people with a smile and some much-needed tenderness. I remember a trainee doctor once telling me she was going to start asking her colleagues how they were, and then wait for the answer, because 'that never happens around here'. That's kindness in action. Kindness practised at home and with our family and friends always boosts connection and love. Who doesn't love some kindness? Flowers? Yes, please!

## Definition of compassion

My view of compassion is that it goes one giant step further and it doesn't always appear kind. I know that seems hard to fathom, but stay with me while I explain.

So what is compassion? Paul Gilbert and Kunzang Choden in their book *Mindful Compassion* say this:

> *Compassion is not just about kindness or 'softness' and it is certainly not a weakness, it is one of the most important declarations of strength and courage known to humanity. It is difficult and powerful, infectious and influential. And, crucially, is perhaps the only universally recognised language with the ability to change the world.*[1]

The word compassion literally means 'to suffer with'. When we act with compassion, we stay the distance. Dr Kieran Sweeney, a highly respected UK doctor who was diagnosed with malignant mesothelioma wrote extensively about his personal experience. Sweeney said this:

> *Thus I am dispatched to the kingdom of the sick permanently and irretrievably. This can never be a pleasant journey, but*

*it can be made at least tolerable, dignified, even. One's guides in this world have a dual role: to read the map and direct you accordingly, but also to be with you on the terrain, a place of great uncertainty.*[2]

I am always so struck by this 'calling in' to healthcare workers: you are a guide and your job is to read the map and guide the patient; and be with them on the terrain.

Many times workers say to me, 'I'm too exhausted for compassion' or 'I don't have time for compassion.' I hear you. As I write this chapter, much of the world continues to be caught in the grip of a fierce pandemic, a terrifying resurgence of the Taliban in Afghanistan and the climate change catastrophe. You have every reason to feel despair. You can own that. This book isn't about positive affirmations or fake joy. So many of us are right up at the frontline. Maybe you feel like you can't tread water much longer. Maybe you long to float for a while until dry land is in sight once more.

If you're tired, worn down or feel unseen and you need to do one less thing, I implore you don't let compassion be the thing you let go of. Hold on and let compassion be your life preserver. Let it show you how to see the distress and stay present. Your *Self* needs you to give it some compassion, your *Self* needs you to find time to feed it and give it water.

Your broken organisation needs compassion. It needs you to see the distress, the tiredness, the fear and the struggle and to set about bringing in some love.

Put very simply:

**Compassion is a sensitivity or awareness to suffering or distress, in ourselves and others, with a commitment to try and alleviate and prevent it.**

Let's read that again. Compassion is a sensitivity to suffering or distress in self. Yes, in yourself – not just in others. Most of us have spent our lives thinking that compassion was exclusively about other people. You need to count yourself in. In Chapter Four we will give self-compassion our full attention.

Compassion is a skill, not a feeling or an emotion. Compassion has a set of steps that require deliberate attention and response. Most importantly, compassion is a verb. It requires action. Compassion always drives you to take action to alleviate the distress in yourself and in others. This is not always easy; in fact, it often feels like hard work. It's the hard emotional labour of showing up and speaking up.

When we have incompetent or poorly skilled leaders operating in positions of authority in our organisation, it is the compassionate response for those with organisational oversight or governance responsibilities to have frank and fearless conversations with them. I see the fall-out of bad behaviour at a very senior level far too often. I've heard people described as 'a bit prickly' or 'their bark is worse than their bite'. This minimising of incivility, micro aggressions and harassment has to stop. It is the opposite of compassion to ignore these inefficiencies, to take the easier route, not the brave one.

When we see that the budget is overspent by hundreds of millions of dollars and is not likely to reset and all the threats and demands that the funder is making are futile, someone with courage and compassion has to speak truth to power.

In this way, I see compassion as both the driving force and the touchstone of healthcare. Anyone who has been seriously ill knows that it is compassion, thoughtfulness and sensitivity on the part of healthcare staff that make it possible to cope with the panic and indignity of a failing body. Anyone who has ever worked in a healthcare organisation knows it is compassionate leadership that rises up with strength and power and shines a light so we can all stay together and survive the storm. This is the very thing we have all been yearning for during the global pandemic from political leaders across the world. Compassion is both these things: it is the light touch and the firm hand.

## The difference between empathy and compassion

Empathy is another example of a term often misunderstood. We might think that empathy is the same as compassion, but it's not. Empathy might kickstart compassion, so you have a sense of understanding what another person is feeling and you are able to feel that, too. But it's not the same as compassion and there are flaws in relying entirely on empathy. In his book *Against Empathy: the case for rational compassion* Paul Bloom uses the devastating school shooting at Sandy Hook Elementary School in Newtown, Connecticut, to demonstrate the way unchecked empathy works.[3] A wave of empathy across the United States was directed at Newtown, Connecticut from people who felt the pain of this tragedy. So what did they do? They started to send toys and gifts. Even when the Mayor said, 'Please, don't send anything else,' still the gifts and toys came. They had to recruit volunteers to sort through thousands of toys that were not needed. The gifts kept coming. They had to build new warehouses to store the steady stream of fluffy bears and Lego sets that were never going to be of any material use to the town. Newtown, Connecticut is a reasonably affluent part of America and the monetary donations were coming from some of the poorest parts of the United States. They were accumulating millions of dollars that the town didn't necessarily need. It didn't alleviate their distress – it started to cause more distress. This is where empathy without compassion leads us.

Bloom's definition of empathy versus sympathy is one of the most simple I have found.

*If you feel bad for someone who's bored, that's sympathy. But if you feel bored, that's empathy. If you feel bad for someone in pain, that's sympathy. But if you feel pain, that's empathy.*[4]

That's the difference between empathy and sympathy, but what about compassion?

Compassion can be fierce. It can be radical. It can be the axe that breaks down the door of racial inequality. It can stand up against bullying and harassment in the workplace, and it can be this kind and loving balm when people need that to meet the distress that they're feeling.

## SUMA

There are four steps in every compassionate action. I call these steps SUMA. You don't have to count them out or make a conscious effort to follow them in strict order. I want you to think of them like breathing effectively where you take refreshing oxygen deep into your lungs, exercising your diaphragmatic muscles and at the same time relaxing your body. The in-breath isn't any more important than the out-breath. We don't have to remind ourselves to exhale before we inhale. At each breath the oxygenated blood courses through our body. This happens whether we think about it or not. SUMA works in the same way. As you begin to cultivate the conditions for compassion you will notice the flow.

The four steps of compassion, SUMA, are:

- Show up
- Understand
- Move closer
- Act.

Let me unpack these steps for you.

*Every day we can practise coming back to the present moment.*

*We remain curious about what others are experiencing and begin to recognise everyone's story is complex and there are many pathways forward.*

*When things go wrong we have a perfect opportunity to move closer. This is your invitation to celebrate our shared humanity.*

*Compassion is a verb and it demands action. This is the step where we powerfully connect with others from a place of vulnerability.*

# Step One: Showing up

*To pay attention, this is our endless and proper work.*

*Mary Oliver*

The next moment isn't going to be any more exciting, revealing or important as the moment you are in right now. We show up big when we realise the wonder and opportunity of the place where we are right now. The place is called Here. This is the gig. Every day we can practise coming back to the present moment. Sharon Salzberg teaches us that the healing is in the return. We foolishly think that the reward is always in the continued unhindered progress. But the truth is that every time we begin again, every time we return to ourselves, we are right where we need to be.

Before you can notice distress – yours or someone else's – you need to be present and show up in the room. Two Harvard psychologists, Killingworth and Gilbert, used a special iPhone Track Your Happiness app to gather 250,000 data points on their subjects' thoughts, feelings and actions as they went about living their lives.[5] They found that people spend 46.9 per cent of their waking hours thinking about something other than what they're doing, and this mind-wandering typically makes them unhappy. Think about this – almost half of the time, you are thinking about something completely unrelated to the action you are carrying out and it is making you miserable. Unlike Fido, your pet dog, you are busily contemplating events that happened in the past, might happen in the future or may never happen at all. This mind-wandering appears to be the human brain's default mode of operation.

Even now as you are reading this book, your mind is wandering and returning. Did I turn off the iron? Am I doing the pick-up tomorrow? Where did I read about asters and goldenrods as complimentary plants? Our mind drifts, our attention follows, and we get lost. We find ourselves wandering aimlessly and we bring ourselves home. This is the essence of mindfulness. Our mind wanders and we bring it home without any judgement. It is a training in staying with where we are right now. Mindfulness meditation is a practice where we devote some time each day to bring ourselves home. Later in this chapter we will talk about how to do a simple mindfulness meditation where we pay attention to our breath, as a way of bringing ourselves back to the here and now. I like to think of it as bringing ourselves in from the cold.

Mihaly Csikszentmihalyi (pronounced mee-high chik-sent-mee-high), a Hungarian-American psychologist, recognised and named the psychological concept of *flow*. Remember the last time you felt you were in flow state? Time seemed to pass more quickly, you were absorbed in the activity and your thinking was focused and directed on what you were doing. Maybe you were reading to a small child, playing the cello or working on your thesis. You felt happy and productive. You showed up. You were at one with the work and everything seemed to unfold with ease.

In Japan they have a concept called *yutori* that explains this idea of showing up and being in the present moment. When we need to be somewhere or be with someone, we take a moment just before that meeting starts or just before the person arrives to pay attention. In Japan, if you travel to a meeting, you may turn up three minutes earlier so that you can notice the thick black bark of the pine tree towering 30 metres above your head. You might see that the sky is clear and there are starlings in the distance. Ah, 'I have arrived,' you will say to yourself.

We don't have to be in Japan to practise yutori. But we have to take a couple of minutes to show up. There's an exercise that I do at the beginning of all of my Compassion Labs where we still ourselves for a moment, settle our breathing and say hello to right now.[6] Maybe you are sitting in an old meeting-room where the curtains don't close properly: hello. Or you feel a rumbling hunger in your belly: hello. You might be reading this page in your favourite chair and you feel warm with the expectation of what will happen next. Whatever it is, we notice it and we say hello. We can say hello to being frustrated, being happy, being sad and being tired. Start saying hello to whatever it is that is happening for you.

> *I say hello to chaos, my unmade decisions, my unmade bed, my desire and my trouble. I say hello to distraction and privilege. I greet the day and I greet my beloved and bewildering Jesus. I recognise and greet my burdens, my luck, my controlled and uncontrollable story. I greet my untold story, my unfolding story, my unloved body, my own body. I greet the things I think will happen and I say hello to everything I do not know about the day. I greet my own small world and I hope that I can meet a bigger world that day.[7]*
>
> *Pádraig Ó Tuama*

This small practice helps me to be in the present moment, even if just for a few moments. I say hello like this many times throughout the day. It also helps me to know what I am feeling. Hello to all the new things we are learning about our colleagues by virtue of all the Zoom meetings in their homes, in our pyjama pants with our work shirts on. Say hello to everything.

You might be thinking, 'There is so much distress that if I start noticing it, I'm going to be overwhelmed. I'm never going to come out from under the doona.' You don't have to notice all the distress. In Step One we are simply showing up, being present and taking notice of what is happening right in front of our eyes. It's not like doomsday scrolling at the beginning of COVID-19, when everyone seemed to be reading one news article, then another, then scrolling and finding yet another. Soon 30 minutes had gone by and you'd have read all these terrible news reports about Italy and France, and how the emergency wards and the ICUs were full and no one could keep up. No wonder you were exhausted.

I bet you wish that you'd known then that showing up and being where you are now – not off doomsday scrolling or thinking about what has happened and what might happen – would have been far less exhausting. We're not thinking about all of the things that happen in all of the world because we can't possibly attend to them. We're thinking about where we are now, what we are doing and how we can be fully there. Sometimes people tell me that they have ten things going on in their lives at the same time. Their father is going into hospital; their son is having panic attacks about his end-of-year exams in lockdown; their neighbour just had a baby and is all alone and to top it all off, the mortgage payment is due. 'How can I pay attention to all of them?' You can't. You can worry about all of them, you can feel a low rumbling anxiety about all of them and stay awake at night with a loop tape playing that has you full of dread. You can set your life up to be continually distracted by your list of things crying out for your attention but you can't notice all of them in a way that brings relief.

The practice of showing up isn't going to bring an end to all the distress swirling around you. Step One is a practice of seeing what is happening right where you are. When we are anxious, we are scanning for distress. But it is unhelpful and it is a diversion that keeps us from showing up. I know this might sound counter-intuitive, so bear with me for a little longer.

I've had this realisation so many times in my life. It's not like you discover this and you're done. I've had times when I honestly felt that if I stopped pedaling, the world would stop spinning. If I didn't jump up and do more, it wouldn't get done. Who was I kidding? We are surrounded by others and our job is to be fully present and awake.

We can't manage the suffering in Afghanistan or the global pandemic or the precarious financial situation of our best friend. All we can do is be here, now. When we are with our father who is unwell, we can be fully with him. Some of the most profoundly beautiful moments in my life have been short lived. Remember the last time you felt fully seen by someone, maybe for just five full minutes. With practice, showing up and being right where you are, can feel effortless and yet it has enormous impact.

Many years ago, I was very unwell. I could barely lift my head off the pillow with muscle pain and inflammation. Lots of people phoned me, anxiety in their voice, checking in again to see if I had improved. For as long as I could, I managed their anxiety, knowing they loved me and took their calls, until one day I decided that I couldn't carry this responsibility any longer. My calls were diverted to my partner. He would deliver messages, filtered of all the noise. 'Sue called. You are so loved.' One day, there was a knock at my front door and there stood my dear friend Sandi, smiling and filled with good cheer. 'Hello Goddess, I've come to rub your feet.' I laid back on the sofa and fell into a light sleep while Sandi massaged my toes. Then as if it were a dream, she was gone. This has stood out for me as the most wonderful example of being present and bringing love into the room. Let's #BeMoreLikeSandi.

The Buddhist teacher Pema Chödrön wrote in her book *When Things Fall Apart:*

> *We don't set out to save the world; we set out to wonder how other people are doing and to reflect on how our actions affect other people's hearts.*[8]

Your job is not to make all the pain go away. Don't make a sign to wear that reads, 'Hello, I'm a Compassion Revolutionary, and my job is to notice your distress and spend my life alleviating it.' Your job is not to heal the world or to save everyone – that's not the work of a Compassion Revolutionary. That is the misguided work of an ego out of control or anxiety left to run untamed.

You need boundaries. Shannon Weber, the author of *Show Up Hard*, talks about this idea of being a 'boundary ninja' – knowing where your boundaries are and being clear about them.[9] When you're clear, other people can be clear too. It's up to you how you set your boundaries and how you maintain them. It also gives you all that room inside the boundary to completely show up.

## Step Two: Understanding

One of my favourite words from the *Dictionary of Obscure Sorrows* is *sonder*.

> *sonder n. the realization that each random passerby is living a life as vivid and complex as your own—populated with their own ambitions, friends, routines, worries and inherited craziness—an epic story that continues invisibly around you like an anthill sprawling deep underground, with elaborate passageways to thousands of other lives that you'll never know existed, in which you might appear only once, as an extra sipping coffee in the background, as a blur of traffic passing on the highway, as a lighted window at dusk.[10]*

Sonder describes the moment where you start to see the other person as having a life as complex and intricate as your own. You are not the central character in their lives, at best you are an extra, merely sipping coffee in the background. You have the same worries, anxieties and fears.

I facilitated a Compassion Lab a couple of years ago – things were going well, the group seemed to be connecting and we were moving into the session on self-compassion. I noticed one particular participant, a quiet woman in her early twenties, taking lots of notes but not really contributing yet to the unfolding Lab. Each time I looked over towards her, I noticed that she was whispering to her colleague with her hand cupped near her mouth. She would whisper and he would smile or nod or shrug. I imagined that she was finding flaws in the Lab design or maybe my voice was boring her. Maybe I reminded her of someone or maybe she simply wasn't a big fan of compassion. I got a little irritated by the story I was telling myself. I started to ignore the whispering woman. I rarely glanced her way.

At the conclusion of the Lab, people were thanking me and expressing their gratitude for the things they had learned throughout the day. The young woman was waiting to speak to me. I approached, curious to hear her reflections. As I came closer, I noticed for the first time that she had a pronounced scar from an orofacial cleft (cleft lip) and she had developed an anxious habit of covering her mouth when she spoke. The Whispering Woman was called Zahair and she wanted to tell me that she had experienced a profound realisation about compassion throughout the day and had taken lots of notes. With her small hand shielding her scar, she said, 'I kept thinking of new ways we could use these ideas back at the hospital.'

I needed to drop the story. You also have a catalogue of stories that you tell yourself and these stories determine how you will respond in any given situation. These appraisals of behaviour will open up or shut down the path to compassion. When you remain curious and take steps to inquire about what others are experiencing, you start to see that the story is complex and there are many pathways forward. Curiosity drives us to ask others, 'How can I help?' and 'What am I missing here?'

Monica Worline and Jane Dutton in their book *Awakening Compassion at Work: The Quiet Power That Elevates People and Organisations* define appraisals that awaken compassion as 'generous interpretations of suffering.'[11] You can cultivate these generous appraisals by having a positive default position that people who experience distress and suffering are good and they are deserving of compassion, not blame. In this way, you build up your ability to notice where suffering is masked by missed deadlines, failures, absences at work, over-eating, avoidance and lack of care. When you are open to seeing suffering, you will notice it hidden behind all manner of behaviours.

I worked with a woman, Sylvia, many years ago who sometimes looked a little bit dishevelled and tired. She was falling behind in her work and we all wondered if she was unwell. From time to time, we asked her, 'Are you okay?' We were nervous about taking it much further when she responded, 'Yes, I'm fine.' Her line-manager gave Sylvia a warning: things need to improve or performance management will commence.

One day a staff member went into Sylvia's office and quietly closed the door behind her. 'Sylvia, is everything okay at home? How is your heart feeling? I am worried about you.' Sylvia started to cry. It turned out that she didn't have a safe home to go to and had started sleeping in the office. Right here in the place I worked, a middle-aged woman was sleeping in her office and I had no idea. Her pain and distress were masked by the deteriorating quality of her work and her lack of concentration. The colleague who went to Sylvia's office and gently spoke with her was making a generous appraisal of the suffering she had noticed. This appraisal meant that Sylvia was seen as good and worthy and in need of help.

One of the most disturbing things I notice in organisations where compassion is thin, is that staff begin to develop a passivity to care.

The whole organisation develops antibodies to trust. The default position is 'don't let your guard down, it's not safe'.

In Chapter Six we will dive deeper into the ways we can build the architecture of compassion into our organisations. But for now, listening is everything. You can practise listening with a great deal of curiosity and fascination. When you're listening, don't assume that you know the answer. Suspend your judgement. Give people the benefit of the doubt. Be curious about how their distress may have arrived, how it might be resolved, why people are feeling the way they feel and what may have contributed to it.

Ask lots of questions to open up your field of view.

Why do we do it this way? What am I missing? Help me fall in love with your idea. How can I help? What matters to you? What are we hoping to build here? What if? Who isn't in the room?

Be mindful to form questions that don't invite blame into the room. We ask, 'what happened to you?' rather than 'what is wrong with you?'; 'what will help right now?' rather than 'why didn't you call sooner?' We acknowledge that our knowledge is only a small part of the collective wisdom in the room and we ask others to help us understand the wider picture. These shifts in enquiry help us to understand what is happening underneath the problem or situation, deep down into the anthill of possibilities.

You might get it wrong. You might try to make sense of what is happening and be off the mark. But you will get better at it the more you do it and if you stay open and curious, people will give you lots of generous feedback.


## Step Three: Move closer

When we come to Step Three we have a choice – avert our eyes and pretend we don't see the distress or move closer and recognise that we are all connected through our shared humanity. The more we move closer the more we will want to do it.

The short-beaked echidna has the largest prefrontal cortex relative to body size of any mammal, taking up 50 per cent of the volume. Who knew? Obviously, you're not an echidna, but your prefrontal cortex is responsible for your ability to plan, make decisions and think about complex ideas. You are able to moderate your social behaviour, to express your personality and to work with efficiency. You can also distance yourself from whatever is happening. You can avoid certain feelings by turning your attention away from what is happening. We've all done this. We see a homeless person sleeping on the sidewalk and we cross the street. Why do we cross the street? Because we want to put distance between ourselves and whatever we find unpleasant. We do this with ourselves habitually. We see those parts of ourselves that we don't want to make friends with, so we avert our eyes, we get busy, we work harder or we fall asleep. Moving closer is realising that this very moment, the one we are in right now, is a perfect teacher. We can move close-in to our beautiful and miraculous but very ordinary lives. Moving closer means staying with that shakiness – or as Pema Chödrön would say

> *... we stay with a broken heart, with a rumbling stomach, with the feeling of hopelessness and wanting to get revenge ... sticking with that uncertainty, getting the knack of relaxing in the midst of chaos, learning not to panic – this is the spiritual path. Getting the knack of catching ourselves, of gently and compassionately catching ourselves, is the path of the [revolutionary].*[12]

This keeps us humble. We see others mess up, fall down, drop the ball, make a fool of themselves and we take a small step toward them.

Sometimes when we see wretchedness, we can use it as a reminder that we wake up, our breath smells, our hair is unruly, maybe we have stubble on our chin and we've slopped some tea on our top. We yawn and stagger to the bathroom. It's all very ordinary just like everyone else. This is the stuff we have in common with everybody. We're all just coming out of the same dream and telling ourselves it's different.

When things go wrong we have a perfect opportunity to move closer. In many organisations the default response to error is to find the person to blame. Everyone starts to move away and defend their actions. By extending compassion and not blame, we can learn from our collective mistakes. We are never going to achieve a workplace free from error. Systems have the potential for error built into them. When we apply a compassionate approach, we start to build strength and competence in our people rather than constraining them in order to avoid error.

High reliability organisations like aviation, military, transportation and health operate at optimal level when they are pre-occupied with failure. Across the organisation they understand that failure, error and near-miss is where they learn and improve and prevent catastrophic accidents. They analyse root cause without blame on people, in fact people who report near misses/failure are actively rewarded. Leaders actively seek warnings of potential for error and communicate openly with front-line staff. This is the level of mindfulness we need at work because significant accidents or catastrophes never happen as the result of one major unforeseen event. They happen because of multiplied small errors and oversights. They keep happening when organisations don't embed a blame-free culture.

The *Titanic* sank because there was a thermal haze causing an optical illusion on the horizon on the night that it sunk. Vikings called these apparent fog banks *Hafgerdingar*, meaning 'sea hedges'. They are not unusual.

The haze was a clear warning sign that significant icebergs were present but it also created an optical illusion leading to the misjudgement of the distance and depth of the 200 metre iceberg. The lookouts didn't report the haze because they thought it was immaterial and because they didn't report it, the *Titanic* missed the warning sign that danger was very close by. This happens over and over again in organisations across the world. What does this have to do with compassion? People see small anomalies and discount them because they are not empowered to speak up, no one listens or they fear ridicule, blame or mistrust.

Moving closer is your invitation to be brave. Many years ago, I heard a little boy of about six say to his three-year-old sister who had fallen over, 'Come on, you can find your brave.' It's a message I've taken into my life. We can reach in knowing that we've been able to do hard things before, and we'll be able to do them again. When you shrink away, think about that little boy and how you might find your own brave.

## Step Four: Act

More than anything else, compassion is about alleviating distress and suffering. It is a verb and it demands action. How do we act? We showed up, we made some intelligent guesses about what was happening so that we could arrive at a clearer understanding and we're willing to move in closer. Now we have to do something.

Warning: this step is not about yoga mats.

If we don't attend to the first three steps, we end up acting without compassion and sometimes without intelligence. Anyone who works in an organisation where the workload is grinding and the hours are long knows that we're going to need a lot more than chocolate iced donuts on a Friday. We can't Krispy Crème our way out of distress and burnout. When your organisation is heading for a monumental overspend and the ambulances are ramping up outside the Emergency Department because the system cannot complete timely discharge and has no capacity to receive any further patients until the bottleneck has eased, you need clarity, emotional tenacity and the will to make a difference. Holding on, getting up the next day and going back to work is compassion in action. Taking a day off to rest up is also compassion in action.

The willingness to act, to actually do something, is what separates compassion from kindness. This is the step where we connect powerfully with others from a place of vulnerability. But in the face of all that is needed you may wonder where on earth you would start and how you would ever find the end. Often, we are called upon to do things that unintentionally cause pain and distress. The COVID-19 pandemic has meant that many palliative care, emergency and intensive care workers have not been able to allow family members to come in and be with their relatives at the end of life. I have heard, firsthand, stories of the creative ways these health care workers have responded by introducing iPads so families could see and speak with the ones they love; all the extra phone calls that have been made to keep families up to date because no visitors were allowed. I've heard about health care workers sitting with people holding their hands and singing to them as they took their last breath.

Many workers pasted a smiling casual photograph of themselves onto their personal protective gown because they knew that patients couldn't see their faces and they wanted them to know they were being cared for by a real human being with a big smile and unruly hair. People found ways of being able to act, even though they were limited in their capacity.

A few months ago as I was preparing to speak on a panel discussion about Moral Injury, I received a private message on

Twitter. A junior doctor had messaged me out of sheer desperation.

*Hi Mary. Feel a bit silly reaching out like this. But, I'm not sure where to go for advice. I am a relatively junior consultant thrown into a senior position in one of the most under-resourced areas … in the state. The overwhelming workload, moral injury and burnout factor is kind of off the scale and paralysing me.*

I'd like to say that this was a once-off, but I get messages much like this every week. These are distressed and desperate professionals who feel isolated and exhausted. The shocking part is not that this doctor feels this way, it's that there is no one in her organisation that she feels she can safely reach out to for help. She wants to pass her exams and keep her job and she wants to do well. She most likely asks herself, 'what is wrong with me? Why am I drowning?'

I can't possibly fix the broken system that she works in, I can't even promise her a reasonable workload. But I can act with compassion. This is what I did:

I sat still for a moment and read her message. I gave it my full attention as I absorbed the content. I understood from her message exactly where she worked and the strain that her department was under. I allowed myself to tune into how distressing it can feel when you are completely overwhelmed. I recalled the visceral sensations that I experience when I am exhausted and overwhelmed; the trembling, hot and prickly feel of my skin; the fuzzy claustrophobic sensation in my head when my limbic system is upregulated; the constant doubt that will plague me; the lead weight I seem to carry around with me. Then I reached out to my network of senior doctors and asked if there was anyone who would be available to give this woman a call so she knew she was not alone. Very quickly I heard from two doctors, both willing to call her. I asked the junior doctor if I could pass on her phone number and she thanked me for being there and was relieved to know someone had heard her call for help.

Then I tapped my heart as a signal to myself that the cycle was finished.

This entire act of compassion took less than five minutes and I went on with my preparations and joined the panel for a powerful discussion that was made richer by my exchange of messages moments earlier.

## Tapping the heart-space

My final gesture of tapping my chest at about the place where I imagine my heart sits is important and I want to give you a little context about this action. Touching or tapping my heart signals to my body that the act of compassion has come to an end. It finishes the work. This is the way you can come back to the present moment. You can do this many times every day, showing up and touching your heart.

Sometimes this is Step Four of compassion. It is the act and the return. When I make this gesture, I relax my nervous system. Airports and crowded shopping centres are great places to notice the full spectrum of reactions and emotions. Perhaps you notice a parent speaking harshly to a small child, or someone looking stressed or lost. You can flow through the four steps in an instant and all anyone will see is your hand gently touching your chest. We can offer this as the act of compassion and smile or nod our head at the person we are directing love and compassion towards. It can be a small gesture that says, 'I see you'.

These steps do not require you to visibly engage with anyone but yourself. Your heart is the project you are working on. Sometimes when I'm feeling brave and I see someone getting cross and speaking harshly to whoever is on the other end of their mobile phone, I allow myself to acknowledge that what I am really looking at is the mirror. That's me, right there, leaking anxiety and managing it the best way I know how. Sure, I'd probably eat some chocolate biscuits or overwork instead of shouting, but it all comes from the same place – fear.

Not everything I notice is distressing. More often than not I see things that cause my heart to gently swell with happiness. I remember standing at the corner of Bourke and Elizabeth Streets in Melbourne, waiting for the lights to change, aware that a man standing next to me carried a small child on his shoulders. The child was absent-mindedly curling the man's hair around his tiny fingers, over and over again. I can still feel the happiness and warmth that welled up inside me. Without even thinking, my hand reached out of my pocket and touched my heart. It was as if I was turning to my own self and saying, 'look how beautiful life is'. These are the moments that sustain and nourish us.

# Compassion muscle workout

## Meditation practice

You might feel like you can't meditate. Maybe you've tried to meditate before and it didn't work out. I'm not a meditation person, you say.

Remember the gym. Maybe you signed up and you set the alarm. Maybe you even posted a pic on Insta of you and the new training gear. When you got to the gym, you couldn't lift weights and you didn't know the routine and it was cold at 6:00 in the morning. After two sessions, you said, 'I'm not a gym person.' The difference between you and a gym person is that the gym person keeps going. That's all it is. It's about growing a muscle.

Make your goal for this week is to sit in a chair that you have designated as your meditation chair. Place both feet on the floor, straighten your back, rest your hands in your lap, close your eyes and simply say quietly in your mind – here I am. Breathe in and breathe out. Stretch and get up. Meditation is over. All you need to do tomorrow is return.

Be kind to yourself, let yourself off the hook and create a practice. The compassion muscle will grow, I assure you.

## Mindfulness meditation

Mindfulness is simply paying attention to the present moment (the moment where the body and the breath reside) without any judgement. Mindfulness meditation is a practice that you can use to train your mind to return and stay in the present moment. If you have ever had a puppy, you will know how tricky return and stay training can be. But you don't smack the puppy or growl at the puppy when you are teaching him to stay. You simply say 'stay' and the puppy wanders and you bring the puppy back and you say 'stay'. This is the way I learnt to meditate 32 years ago at the instruction of Pema Chödrön. I would listen to a cassette tape of Pema teaching me to stay. It has served me well over all these years.

Sharon Salzberg, the renowned loving kindness meditation teacher, tells the story of the very first time she meditated. She sat down in preparation and thought to herself, 'okay, how many breaths will it be before my mind drifts?' She naively thought she would probably only make it to 800. She was wrong. By the first breath her mind had wandered off, just like the puppy. Don't be disheartened, the mind wanders.

Meditation is a training exercise. My little granddaughter learned to walk five months ago. She didn't get up one day and walk into the kitchen and astound us. She learned to walk through practice. She didn't judge herself or compare herself to other walkers. She got up on her feet and fell down. She laughed and tried again. One day she noticed that if she held onto something she could shift her weight from one foot to the other. That's cool, she probably thought as she plopped down again. This is exactly how we learn to practise mindful meditation. We find a comfortable place to sit, we don't need to wear a shawl or have a cushion or cross our legs or burn incense or eat ghee (although all of those things are fine, too). We simply sit down with ourselves and settle into a position where we feel stable and experience minimal distraction. You can sit in a chair or on the floor or you can lie down on a firm surface. Whatever works for you. Set a little timer for five or ten minutes to start with and see how you go.

## The practice

Step 1. Sit or lie down in a comfortable position.

Step 2. Set your timer for five or ten minutes.[13]

Step 3. Take a moment to notice your body. Relax and notice any sensations in your body. Are you feeling tight across your shoulders or tight inside your chest? Just notice what's happening inside your own body – you know, the one that is in the present moment with you.

Step 4. Feel your breath coming in and out through your nose. You might like to count each breath. Breathing in and then breathing out you count 'one' and continue with the next repetition.

Step 5. Soon your mind will wander. It is inevitable. Your mind wants to go to other places. Maybe it happens at the first breath or after a few seconds or a minute or two. No big deal. Simply return to the next breath.

Step 6. Quietly say to yourself 'stay' and bring your mind back to the breath. No drama, you are simply observing and training. You can start counting again. Breathing in and then out you say 'one'. You will remember things that you have to do, places you have to be. This is normal. Don't give your thoughts too much attention. Just notice them and come home.

Step 7. Finish with kindness towards yourself. You can finish your meditation with a short prayer. May I be well. May I be happy. May I be free from harm.

Open your eyes and notice what is happening around you, take in the sounds and the smells.

You have spent time in the present moment. Remember: no judgment. You don't need to give your meditation a score out of ten.

## Create a SUMA practice

Now that you understand how SUMA works, let's create a practice.

Today I want you to take a few minutes and bring yourself into the present moment.

What do you notice when you stop and see what is happening right where you are?

What do you hear?

Give yourself to this moment. Quietly say to yourself, I am here. I have arrived.

## Conclusion

Now we know what compassion is and how to act with compassion, we're going to take a look at the science of compassion. Our brain and our nervous system are responsible for a lot of our distress, but the good news is we can calm and soothe ourselves, and we can calm and soothe others. Even better than that, we can change our brain, and in the next chapter I'm going to show you how.

# 3

# The science of compassion

*The way out of the storm and mud of suffering, the way
back to freedom on the high edge of strength and courage, is
through the power of compassion.*

*Joan Halifax*

My mind is not so much a temple as an amusement park.

It chatters and hums almost constantly. I don't write this chapter because I lean towards the Zen. I write because I've slept with my smartphone! I've checked emails secretly under the restaurant table while having a meal with people I really care about. I once went out for coffee with my partner on a lazy Sunday morning. I had completely forgotten he was there while I frantically answered text messages. I was gently returned to the present moment when I received a text message from him: *would you like to have coffee with me?*

If you're like me, you live a fast-paced life that includes face to face time with other human beings and increasingly more of that time happens via a screen. I go through phases of working too hard and then finding I have reached my edge. I take my foot off the pedal and slow my pace. A bit later in this chapter you will easily guess that routinely my attention is on balancing my Drive and my Soothing Systems.

In early December 2019, before any of us had heard about COVID-19, I wrote this in my journal:

*This week I worked in three different cities, waited in various airports for flights (some delayed) and caught multiple Ubers. I slept, often fitfully, in four different beds, I ate hotel food that I swore I wouldn't eat and was endlessly tempted by mini bars selling chocolate bars at ridiculously inflated prices (I stayed firm for this small victory). I held space for two whole days for 45 people to experience empathy and compassion, I ran a raucous workshop on being disruptive, wrote a keynote and answered endless emails. I shopped at a local market and ate alone most nights. I meditated quietly in hotel rooms and later in a community hall with others. My mind wandered and stayed fixed. I worried about things that will most likely never happen. I felt vulnerable and brave all at the same time. One friend lost her job last week and another lost his mother. My oldest friend became a grandmother again and my youngest had a miscarriage. All in the space of one week.*

My life is not unusual. This is what happens in seven days. Think about the last seven days of your life. There were ups and downs, moments of clarity and moments lost in a blur. While you may not be able to travel, I bet you're going places on that Zoom screen.

This is what it means to be human. You are moving in space continually and you generally find it hard to still your mind for too long. Even now your mind is wandering. You are interrupted constantly and bombarded with information from every source. All around you there are invitations to buy more, do more, want more and work faster.

In this chapter, I'm going to introduce you to your highly evolved and partially flawed brain and the ways it helps and hinders you in regulating your emotions. We're also going to look at the ways that you can change your body and brain – everything from the expression of your genes to the amount of grey matter you have.

I want us to focus on small changes we can make that will bring a big difference. I'm not going to suggest that you move to the Himalayas and take up residence in a cave for three years or start drinking kale smoothies. I'm going to introduce you to things that are hidden in plain sight. Like the way your connection to others has a protective effect in building resilience or the ways that you can respond to threat, whether it's real or imagined, by activating your soothing system. Because when it comes to threat, the human brain doesn't differentiate between what is real and what is imagined.

## We are hardwired to connect

> *The strongest predictor of a species' brain size is the size of its social group. We have big brains in order to socialize.*
> *Matthew Leiberman*

We have a hidden superpower and it is our ability to chemically and electrically synchronise our brains and bodies. Just below the surface we have moments where we see that we are connecting with others and a dynamic change is happening. Remember the last time you were with someone that you really like and you felt your mood lifting by sitting next to them. Or that wonderful moment when you hold a small baby and feel the weight of them relax into your arms, you gently sway and look into their eyes.

There is a whole cocktail of neural and chemical activity happening right in that moment.

As mammals, our evolutionary biological imperative is to connect so that we survive. We are a connected species and when we feel others, we feel ourselves.

We are, in fact, consumed with guessing what other people might be thinking, particularly about us. When we look into the mirror and ask ourselves our own version of 'does my bum look big in this?' we are really asking if other people will look at us and negatively assess our size. When we stand up to speak to a meeting, we are scanning for cues that our audience are interested/appreciative/bored/outraged, depending on the reaction we are after.

Scientist Matthew Leiberman in his book *Social: Why Our Brains Are Wired to Connect* reports that research on fMRI shows that we have two very different networks that support social and non-social thinking and that as one network increases its activity the other tends to quiet down – kind of like a 'neural seesaw'.[1] No sooner have we finished doing some kind of non-social thinking, the network for social thinking comes back on like a reflex – almost instantly. Our brains are wired to reach out and connect. This isn't about being an extrovert or wanting to socialise. Our brains have evolved to help us connect, build relationships and communities. This social thinking is not a flaw but an asset that fosters our capacity to care for one another. Even our brains are built to help us show up and be curious to understand what is happening to others.

Lieberman asks – why would the brain be set up to do this?

> *… [this] reflex prepares us to walk into the next moment of our lives focused on the minds behind the actions that we see*

*from others. Evolution has placed a bet that the best thing for our brain to do in any spare moment is to get ready to see the world socially.*[2]

The Budhist teacher Joan Halifax in her book *Standing at the Edge: Finding Freedom Where Fear and Courage Meet* wrote about Dr Gary Pasternak, the Medical Director of a Mission Hospice and a long-term meditator. In this section of an email he sent to Halifax, we see the way our human heart cracks open as we connect deeply with others and allows compassion to refresh us once again.

*I'm up late admitting patients to the inpatient hospice unit. Just when I think I'm too old for these late nights without sleep, a person in all their rawness, vulnerability and pain lays before me and as my hands explore the deep wounds in her chest and my ears open to her words, my heart cracks open once again ... And this night a sweet 36 year old woman with her wildly catastrophic breast cancer speaks of her acceptance and her hope for her children, and she speaks with such authenticity and authority. And her acceptance comes to me as the deepest humility a person can experience and then again, once again, I remember why I stay up these late nights and put myself in the company of the dying.*[3]

Over the years I have developed little practices that I use to purposefully build on the magic of connection.

When I meet with people I will look into their eyes, not a long awkward stare but a brief holding of their gaze. This is a powerful way of deeply connecting with others. Our brains are built to pick up an enormous amount of information from the human face, especially direct eye gaze, and we do it at lightning speed.

*From the instant we first lock eyes with another person, specialised brain cells spark into action. When we actively engage, we synchronise the social and emotional networks in our brains. This state, which we call interpersonal neural synchronisation (INS) or neural coupling, allows us to transfer not just information, but meaning, delight, fear and aspiration.*

*Fiona Kerr*[4]

I laugh and cry readily with others. This is how I pay respect and honour the beautiful, flawed and abundant reality of being human. I have had transformational moments with others where we were able to surrender to the power of joy and hold onto our sides as we laughed together. Likewise, I have felt myself grow as I sat with people experiencing deep pain and suffering. Sitting quietly and feeling pain together.

Lately I am developing a new practice of pausing and paying respect when people share painful or difficult stories with me. We can so easily get used to hearing about tragedy or difficult decisions or painful encounters.

Often we discount or minimise our own stories in the telling. I'm practising letting people know that I have heard them and I know there is a deeper, more nuanced version of the story held deep inside them that deserves respect. We can do this in a very simple way. We might respond by saying, 'I'm going to pause for a moment and pay respect to the courage/vulnerability/loneliness/resilience contained in what you shared.' Deep listening is not the same as collecting information.

*The reality is that we are bodies born of other bodies, bodies feeding other bodies, bodies having sex with other bodies,*

*bodies seeking a shoulder to lean or cry on. Bodies matter,*
*which is why anything related to them arouses emotions.*[5]
*Frans De Waal*

Often when I think of someone, I send them an SMS. 'Hey, I was sitting here, drinking my jasmine tea and I thought of you' or 'I just saw a tall man lean down to kiss his son's head and I thought of you and the way your heart is so tender.' People have started doing it to me now. I love it. You might find it takes a while to accept that someone could possibly be thinking about you. Right this minute someone, somewhere, is wondering how you are and marvelling at how fortunate they are to know you.

One of the most powerful mantras we can live by is simply this: we all have something that someone else wants, even if it's just our full attention.

Giving our full attention to ourselves or anyone else is dependent on our capacity to regulate our emotions. We need to be able to switch off our radar for threat and bring ourselves calmly into the present moment where everything is happening right in front of our eyes. This is Step One of SUMA.

## Is this a threat?

Understanding how your mind and body work together will give you greater mastery over the circumstances that you find yourself in. If you spend half your time hijacked by your amygdala – that little part that we often refer to as our lizard brain – you won't get the chance to be the awesome human that you were born to be.

Let me illustrate this with a little story about the difference between human beings and other animals on the evolutionary ladder – for instance, zebras. If a zebra is drinking at a waterhole and notices a lion coming through the bushes, the zebra is going to react by fleeing, fighting or freezing. It will probably not fight because it will come off second-best against a lion. It may freeze, if there's enough material for camouflage. But what the zebra is most likely to do is run for its life. If the zebra makes it to safety, its threat system will return to baseline. And that is what makes zebras so different to us.

The zebra experiences a threat, responds to the threat and then, when it knows that it is safe, it comes back to a state of calm. Zebras have a small prefrontal cortex. Humans have a large prefrontal cortex. We find endless ways to maintain a state of threat. Zebras can't ruminate, they can't go over and over the lion story until everyone is tired of hearing about it. Zebras are not able to criticise themselves: what on earth was I doing at a waterhole frequented by lions? I have a family to raise. Zebras don't have the capacity to imagine the worst possible outcome: what if I'd tripped running to safety? The lion would surely have eaten me alive. A zebra is either safe or not safe. All is not lost for us non-zebras.

We have a brain that has developed over thousands of years. I like to think of the brain as our own personal, albeit secondhand, smart phone. The one you'd give your 12-year-old self. You didn't design it, it's not the model you wish you had. It's not exactly fit for purpose and some days it feels more like a Candy Crush machine that makes calls. Occasionally you have to turn it off, wait five seconds before you turn it back on again. It pings, and beeps and buzzes constantly unless you give it very clear instructions. Learning how to ensure your brain can do all the things you need it to do will require understanding how it works and then maybe adding some apps.

Our Emotion Regulation Systems have been shaped by evolution (not by us) and they are both conscious and unconscious. They are the switchboard for a brain that has evolved to ask, in almost any given situation: is this a threat? Yes or no. Whether we are meeting someone for the first time, buying a car, answering a phone call or dealing with our own version of a sabre tooth tiger, our brain wants to know: is this a threat? A call comes into the switchboard (I'm thinking 1970s style plug and cord): is this a threat? Yes. Sympathetic nervous system kicks in and our threat response is activated and we prepare for fight/flight/freeze. Cortisol and adrenaline are released and we experience stress and anxiety. Is this a threat? No. Our parasympathetic nervous system is switched on and we feel at ease. We are able to rest and digest as opiates and oxytocin are released and we experience calm and contentment.

Of course, the level of challenge we encounter in regulating our emotions is highly impacted by:

- experience of trauma
- white supremacy
- capitalism
- adverse events in childhood
- attachment with a primary caregiver in infancy
- our tolerance for arousal.

As you begin to understand how the following three systems affect your emotions, moods and feelings, and help you to process stimuli, you will be better placed to regulate your responses. The good news is that we are not alone. We all have a tricky brain that we did not design, a brain that is powerful and able to handle complex ideas but can also be consumed by worries about the past and predictions for the future that involve imagined worst case scenarios.

# The three systems: Threat, Drive and Soothe

## *Emotional regulation systems*

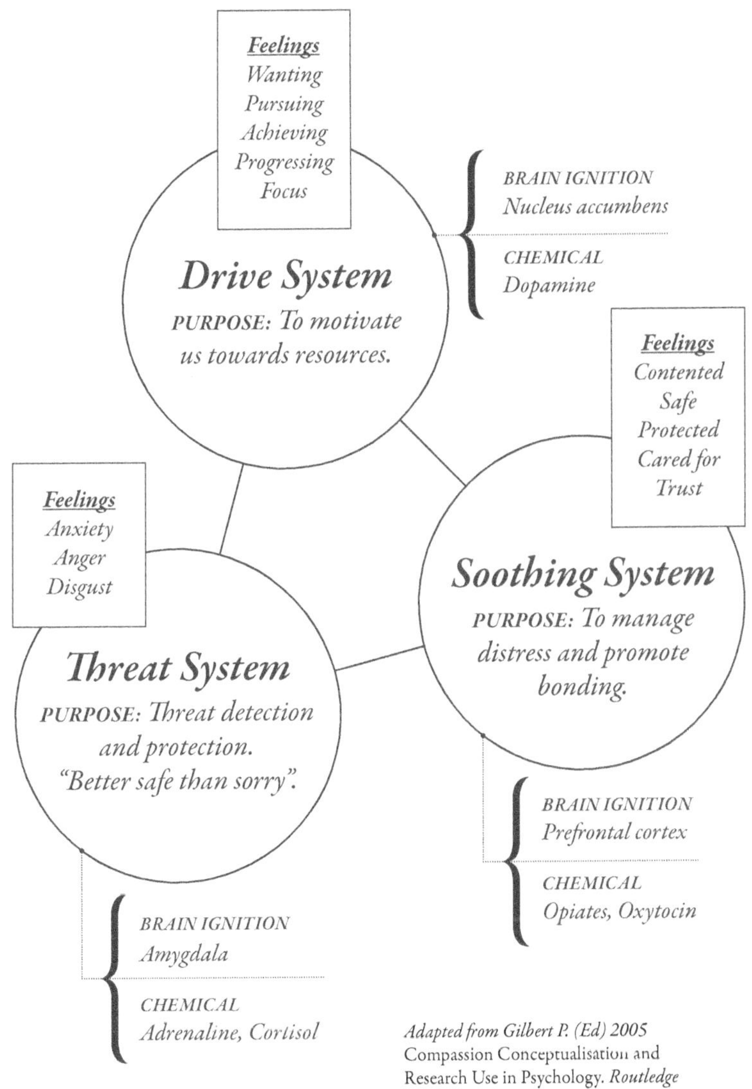


Adapted from Gilbert P. (Ed) 2005 Compassion Conceptualisation and Research Use in Psychology. *Routledge*

These regulation systems are conscious and unconscious. When you are caught in Threat or Drive over an extended period of time, you're not able to be fully present and respond to what is happening in the here or now. You may find that even when you're sitting at your desk and working, you're under a lot of pressure and you haven't noticed that your shoulders are lifting up to your ears. Your neck is starting to get tight. The phone rings, you look down and see the Caller ID, and immediately you feel threatened. You're working on a report that should have been finished an hour ago. You know that people are waiting on it. You look down, see the number and think, 'Oh, no. I'm never going to get this done.' Your heart starts beating faster and you're unable to focus and do the work that you're meant to do. You start to tell yourself a story about how you are letting others down and from there it can be a downhill spiral.

## Threat System – cortisol and adrenaline

The Threat System is the easiest for us to identify because when we experience the threat system in action, we have a number of physiological symptoms. These include increased heart rate, shallow breathing, increased perspiration, feeling of nausea or cramping and tension in our large muscles. The physical sensations can feel overwhelming, and they will cause a fight/flight/freeze response.

The Threat System is powerful and it reacts to the external world – events, actions, incoming information. If a fire alarm goes off in your hotel room in the middle of the night you need a strong and responsive Threat System to get you out of bed and running for the stairs. For people who have been systematically marginalised by white supremacist culture, ableism, discrimination, stereotyping and oppression, the Threat System keeps them alive in a very real and pragmatic sense. Here is another layer of important work for all of us to do in dismantling oppressive structures so that everyone can access the right to feel safe.

I owe a debt of gratitude to the writings of Resmaa Menakem and Layla F. Saad in helping me to understand the role that I play in building safe environments as a white woman in a white supremacist culture.[6] White Supremacy in this context does not refer to neo-nazis or other hate groups. It refers to the everyday assumptions that we make about the centrality of whiteness and the privileges that are accorded to those who live in a white body.

> *[White supremacy is] the all-encompassing centrality and assumed superiority of people defined and perceived as white and practices based on that assumption ... [it] does not refer to individual white people per se and their individual intentions, but to a political-economic social system of domination. This system is based on the historical and current accumulation of structural power that privileges, centralizes, and elevates white people as a group.[7]*
>
> *Robin di Angelo*

Realising that you live in a white supremacist culture and benefit from it every day in a hundred ways can be startling for white bodies. I spent many years allowing a certain tension and irritation that would arise in me when people talked about white privilege to derail any opportunity of being useful in dismantling privilege. Resmaa Menakem's work has helped me hold that tension lightly, let it rise up, and just notice the feelings that arise in my body and watch them pass. I suggest that my white body readers do the same. When you engage in discussion about white privilege (or male privilege or able-bodied privilege) you might notice an irritation or even an urge to be more 'woke'. Let it pass and listen to what your body is trying to tell you. Hard news will generally switch on our Threat System. Practise leaning into it and opening your heart a little wider. This is how we grow compassion. I try to remember the words of the spoken word poet Kyle 'Guante' Tran Myhre – 'white supremacy is not the shark, it is the water'.[8]

Our Threat System also responds to our interior world – memories, thoughts, judgements and predictions. It hardly matters if the threat is real or perceived as our Threat System will respond just as efficiently to both. If you are Black, Indigenous or a Person of Colour, it hardly matters if the police car that drives slowly past you on a side street stops or keeps cruising. Your Threat System has been tuned to anticipate racial profiling and your Threat System is trying to keep you safe.

Our response to threat will differ depending on the circumstances. If someone in authority berates or humiliates you in front of your peers, you might submit (or freeze). Later you might feel a sense of shame or disappointment in your lack of action and from here it is an easy cascade into self-criticism or blame. This keeps the Threat System engaged. Remember you didn't design your own brain, it's not dodgy home repair skills at fault here – this is evolution combined with a potent mix of life events and cultural biases. Nevertheless, we are responsible for the way in which we regulate our emotions and we can train in better efficiency. Road rage is a display of Threat System upregulation. Bullying, blaming, criticism, tantrums, angry outbursts are all displays of a Threat System unchecked.

As a species, humans have evolved to detect threats quickly and to scan for them regularly. This is called 'negativity bias'. It's the reason criticism, bad feedback and insults are felt far more powerfully than compliments and kind words. Recall for a moment your last performance review or a conversation you had with a colleague where they gave you some much needed feedback. What do you remember? We remember the one comment that was negative and we discount all the positive comments. Have you ever read the evaluation comments after facilitating a workshop or giving a presentation? You most likely scanned over 'excellent facilitator', 'great content', 'so valuable' and your eye stopped at 'facilitator did not give enough clear examples'. Suddenly this one comment is highlighted, underscored and illuminated. If I ask you about the workshop you might say, 'they thought my examples weren't clear enough'.

The problem is we can become hijacked by threat and negativity. Of all the skills humans have, our ability to ruminate and imagine the worst outcome is gold medal standard.

## Drive System – dopamine

The Drive System is all about motivation to achieve and accumulate the things we need and want (or think we need). It is centred around doing and acquiring. Our Drive System is useful if we are training for an ultra marathon or embarking on a healthy eating plan. You want to stick to it or you want to improve your time. When we are looking for a promotion our Drive System alerts us to opportunities. Our Drive System offers us the powerful reward of dopamine when we are successful. We often set ourselves small tasks so we can get a little dopamine rush. I'll admit I always include at least two things I have already accomplished on my To Do List. No sooner have I written my list than I've achieved something. Boom! Here comes some dopamine. Maybe you put up a basketball hoop and you spend hours getting the ball in the hoop. Boom! Dopamine.

Sometimes our Drive System goes unchecked and we blindly pursue things that are harmful to us and to others. We may form addictions, compulsive behaviours or work long hours to achieve higher and higher goals. In the animal world we see Drive in action when squirrels collect acorns or magpies collect sticks to build a nest. Now if the magpie attaches his self-worth to his bounty of sticks he would collect sticks all day and night. I just gotta get me some more sticks!

## Soothing System – oxytocin, endorphins and opiates

The Soothing System is also wired into us. It's often referred to as 'rest and digest', and it's this sense of calm and wellbeing that we experience when our Drive and Threat Systems are not in control of our actions. Learning to switch on or upregulate our Soothing System is a powerful practice for turning down the Threat and Drive Systems.

Think of some of the ways that you might soothe a small child. The tone of your voice changes – 'Hey, little buddy', you say as you bend down so you can look into the child's face. If the child is familiar to you, you might gently rub their back or ruffle their hair. You offer words of encouragement and remind them that all is well and they can get back up and continue their game.

This is not all that different to the way we can soothe ourselves and others as adults. When you are feeling a sense of calm, take a moment to recognise that you feel at ease and relaxed. Remind your brain that this is what the Soothing System is good at. The best way to identify this state is when you're doing something you enjoy and it provides feelings of peace and happiness – such as enjoying time with your family or enjoying time with a good book. Even in your work, if you're in flow and you feel like you are working at the pace that suits you, things are coming to you and you're lost in time, that can feel soothing, and your Soothing System is working well.

## What's this got to do with compassion?

Often people ask me, 'What has any of this got to do with compassion?' It's a fair question and the answer is: everything. Compassion, as you remember from Chapter Two, is about noticing the distress that you and others are experiencing. The very first step involved in SUMA is Showing Up. If we are not able to upregulate our Soothing System we will experience anxiety, stress, fear, numbing and we will sabotage our best efforts with self-criticism.

You already know that we all behave in ways that are unhelpful, to ourselves and to others. If you work in a hospital you will be all too familiar with Code Grey, an emergency response to situations of verbal and/or physical aggression or threatening behaviour involving patients, visitors or caregivers.[9] In many cases, I witness patients or their family members struggling to regulate their Threat System coming face to face with hospital staff who are also struggling to manage theirs. They are worried, triggered and feel helpless and the triage nurse is tired, overworked, hungry and thirsty. What happens next is so predictable.

That isn't a Free Pass for rude and aggressive behaviour towards healthcare workers and it certainly doesn't mean that staff should put up with abuse or threats. But it gives us some powerful clues about how we might soothe others and help them to soothe themselves. We might lower our voice and speak with a warm and friendly tone, we could encourage trust that we are doing everything we can (if we are) by being transparent about what is happening right now, what will happen next and how long that will take. We can ask directly, 'What will help you right now?' People cannot see our intention, we need to make that explicit, they can only see our actions and this view is always filtered through years of experience, negative and positive, and by a hundred things that are not even happening in the present moment.

Waiting-rooms send messages and often they shout 'threat' when they could whisper 'soothe'. Maybe now might be a good time to audit the waiting-room your clients/patients/customers are invited to sit in and wait for your attention, often while trying to manage small children and their own failing bodies. At the end of this chapter, I have included a Waiting-room scan. Invite a colleague and a consumer advocate to do this scan with you and then debrief together.

## Threat System antidotes

When our Threat System is activated unnecessarily (the house is not on fire), it helps if we can bring our Soothing System online. There are many neural exercises that help with this.

You can breathe deeply, increasing the length of the out-breath. These longer, slower exhalations will turn off your Threat System and begin to send powerful messages to your body that you are safe.

You can plant your feet firmly on the floor, pushing down a little with your heels. This stabilising action will give you a strong sense of grounding. Standing or walking can activate your pre-frontal cortex and enable you to tap into rational thought.

Extending the duration of phrases, humming, singing or chanting also has a calming effect.

Playing a wind instrument is also helpful.

Reciprocal play, laughing with friends, chatting with others are all-powerful ways to build social intimacy and bring calm.

## Drive System antidotes

When the Drive System is dominating, stop and reevaluate. This is a great time to revisit a soothing activity, something that is calming.

Often your friends or family will notice that your Drive System is in control long before you do. Your partner may suggest that you're not your usual self. Or if you are fortunate enough to have a daughter as wise and outspoken as mine is, she might give you a wake-up call. Twenty odd years ago when my daughter was 11 years old, she came into my home office and watched me, fully focused on my computer screen as I worked on my thesis while the sun shone outside for yet another Sunday. I don't even know how long she was there before I heard a small voice say, 'This. This is really sad.' And then like most wisdom guru 11-year-olds, she quietly got up and left. My Drive System was running my life. While summer came and went and my child learned new games, I was trying to achieve a degree that at the time seemed like the most important thing in the world.

When this happens, it is time to revisit your goals and ask yourself if they're truly aligned with your priorities. More importantly, build in time to play and sing and dance in the kitchen with your kids or your friends or your dogs.

## Soothing System enhancers

It may seem counterintuitive but while the Soothing System is the most pleasurable of all the three, it's also the easiest to ignore. When you notice that you are feeling fearful or anxious, speak to yourself in a calm and soothing voice. Gently stroke your own arms. You probably already do this. Often when we are feeling anxious, we unconsciously run our hands down our arms or rub our hands together.

You can find so many ways to invite your Soothing System to switch on. It's winter where I am at the moment and I'm staying at a beach house and writing this chapter with a view of the ocean. It's warm inside the house and I have a candle burning. I'm drinking lots of water and taking little breaks to stretch. This helps me not to become anxious when the words don't flow and not to become too demanding of myself. It turns off the voice in my head that says, 'You will never finish this book!'

When the soothing system is in gear, nurture it. Take notice of it. When you're feeling calm and peaceful, allow yourself to enjoy it. Say hello to the calm, to the ease and the delight. Practise using warm, compassionate language towards yourself and others, and remember to Show Up so you can enjoy the moment you are in.

This is not like turning on and off a switch. 'Right, I've done that, and I'm not getting the response that I need.' Our bodies are not little machines.

Dr Miriam-Rose Ungunmerr-Baumann introduced the world to the concept of Dadirri.[10] It speaks to the value of deep listening and quiet stillness and has been a part of Aboriginal practice for thousands of years. Dadirri is a powerful way of balancing our Emotion Regulation Systems.

> *When I experienced Dadirri, I am made whole again.*
> *I can sit on the riverbank, or walk through the trees. Even*
> *if someone close to me has passed away. I can find my peace*
> *in this silent awareness. There is no need of words. A big*
> *part of Dadirri is listening ... to be still brings peace. And it*
> *brings understanding. When we are really still in the bush,*
> *we concentrate. We are aware of the anthills, and the turtles,*
> *and the water lilies.*
>
> *Dr Miriam-Rose Ungunmerr-Baumann*[11]

Training in managing your emotions takes time and patience. The best time to practise is right now, whatever you're feeling. You might ask yourself, 'How might I create love and safety for myself?'

Sit still and see what your body tells you. Remember this isn't about being perfect or getting it right. If you need some assistance to make friends with your emotions, you can seek out a Compassion Focused Therapist.

## Breathing and mindfulness meditation

*The further we get away from the body the more everything starts to go wrong.*

*David Malouf*

The good news is that your body knows how to breathe, and unless someone is reading this to you while you are hooked up to an ECMO machine, then you're breathing right at this moment. Breathing and moving will rapidly help you access control over your nervous system and reach your optimal state. Breathing is the only autonomic function that we can control purposefully. You can control your breath to lower your heart rate variability and your blood pressure. You can also breathe your way to becoming more compassionate.

In Western culture, we tend to idolise the power of the mind over the body. But you can use your body to regulate your mind. This becomes vitally important when you're not able to think your way out of a stressful event. In times of stress and anxiety, you can't think your way to calm. Tai chi and yoga come from an ancient tradition where the body moves in specific ways to directly influence our state of mind. We lie in shavasana or corpse pose, our body flat on the mat, our hands upturned, our eyes closed and we breathe, slowly uncurling our central nervous system and calming our mind.

In 2016 I visited New York City and after participating in a full day workshop, I waited in line to have my copy of *The Happiness Track* signed by Dr Emma Seppälä.[12] As she signed my book, we had a short conversation where I talked about the struggle I sometimes have with coming back to the present moment and staying there. Dr Seppälä said something that was life-changing for me, and it's stayed with me since that day – 'your body is always in the present moment.' It was one of those Boom! moments. If we come home to our body, we will come home to the present moment. Your body is always in the present moment. Your breath is always in the present moment. That's why when we set up for a meditation session, we talk about two feet on the floor, noticing that you're breathing in and out or listening for sounds. Everything that our body does, it does in the present moment. Our body doesn't travel to the past and it doesn't exist yet in the future. Being able to tap into this living, breathing body brings us to the present moment.

Belgian psychologist Pierre Phillipot and his team conducted a number of studies where they measured participants' breathing patterns when they experienced certain emotions like sadness, happiness, fear and anger.[13] The research team found that each emotion was associated with a certain breathing pattern. You breathe differently depending on the emotion you are experiencing. When you are fearful you are likely to take shorter, more rapid shallow breaths, when you feel calm your breaths will be deeper and slower. We have incorporated this understanding into our use of language: when we relax, we say 'ahhh!' When we are relieved, we say 'phew!' Laughing and sobbing also have distinct breathing patterns. When you laugh you create longer exhalations. When you sob you take very short inhalations in rapid succession.

The research became more interesting when Phillipot and his colleagues asked participants to breathe in distinct patterns and were able to replicate the correlating emotion. In other words, if I ask you to take long slow breaths and make your exhalations slightly longer than your inhalations, you will begin to feel calm. Go on, try it!

Congratulations, you just controlled your emotional state using your body rather than your mind. Now if you practised a daily routine of breathing exercises, you would normalise your cortisol levels. Breathing reconditions your body to a state of calm. The simplest way I have learned to improve my breathing is to spend a few minutes each day noticing the way I breathe. You can sit comfortably and become aware of how you are breathing. Over time I have discovered that my breathing changes throughout the day, depending on the task and the emotions that I am feeling. This is another way of becoming friends with ourselves.

Breathing is an effective application for those who find it difficult to meditate because of trauma, stress or overactive thoughts. If you're one of those people who finds sitting still and watching your breath difficult, you might like to practise some of the breathing exercises below.

# Compassion Muscle Workout

## Alternate nostril breathing

Alternate nostril breathing is a yogic breath control practice. In Sanskrit, it's known as *nadi shodhana pranayama*. This translates as 'subtle energy clearing breathing technique.' Hilary Clinton wrote in her book *What Happened* that she used alternate nostril breathing to manage her stress and anxiety after the loss at the 2016 election.

1. Sit quietly somewhere where you can give this exercise your attention.
2. Place your left hand in your lap facing palm upwards.

3. Bring your right hand up and place the index and middle fingers between your eyebrows and your thumb on your RIGHT nostril and your ring finger on your LEFT nostril.
4. Take a deep breath in and closing your RIGHT nostril with your thumb, breathe out through your LEFT nostril.
5. Then take a deep breath in through your LEFT nostril, close the left nostril with your ring finger at the end of this inhalation and breath out through your RIGHT nostril.
6. Breathe in deeply and slowly from the RIGHT nostril. Closing the RIGHT nostril with your thumb, exhale through the LEFT nostril.
7. Repeat the full process three or four more times.
8. Start out slowly and practise for about five minutes.

## Square Breathing (also known as Tactical Breathing or Box Breathing)

Square breathing slows our breathing rate, improves our ability to concentrate and is easy to do on the go. This is one of my go-to breathing exercises when other people are around and I am not able to sit quietly. I practise Square breathing throughout the day.

Step 1.

Breathe in through your nose to the count of four, fill your lungs up with air.

Step 2.

Hold the air in your lungs for the count of four.

Step 3.

Exhale through the mouth to the count of four. All the air should be released from your lungs.

Step 4.

Hold the lungs in an empty state for the count of four.

Step 5.

Repeat all the steps for five mins.

The most important and vital thing to remember is not to force your breathing. If holding for the count of four feels uncomfortable take it down to three. I remind everyone in my Compassion Labs that even though this is called Square Breathing it's fine if your breathing looks more like a triangle or a rectangle to commence. This is a chance to make friends with your breathing, not a competition.

Stick with it. Maybe over the period of a week you might touch into a breathing practice for a minute each day. Often, when we start to move or breathe in a new way, it will feel uncomfortable – like deciding that you're going to write with your left hand if you're right-handed.

It will feel weird. You have learned to breathe in a certain way, and now you're going to be creative and learn some different ways.

## Waiting-room scan

Scanning the area where people wait will give you lots of great data about how your organisation or service is experienced by others. Bring a notebook and a pen.

Take a seat where you can quietly and unobtrusively observe what is happening. Settle yourself and say hello to the present moment. When you are ready to commence, look around and listen to any feelings that arise in your body.

Here are some prompts.

Do you feel safe in this room? Do you feel relaxed and comfortable?

What does the room smell like? Is it a pleasant smell? Is it fresh or stale?

If you are seated in a chair, is it comfortable, clean and in good repair?

What does the room look like? Is it tidy/friendly/clinical? How would you describe the room? Are the posters and other information sources still relevant? If there are books or magazines available, are they up to date? Are a range of bodies and cultures represented? Is the room clean? Are the floors and/or walls worn and need of repair? What feelings does this room evoke for you?

What are the sounds you can hear? Are there competing sounds – sirens, announcements and conversations? Could you easily hear if your name was called? Can you hear distressing sounds/playful sounds/angry sounds? If music is playing, is it too loud?

What are the staff doing? Do they look busy? Do they appear approachable? Is it easy to tell who works here and who is visiting? Do staff wear name badges?

If you were thirsty or hungry, could you easily access food and water? How much money would you need? How far would you need to travel to access refreshments?

If you were a small child, what would you do to pass the time? Are there toys or books to play with? What about visual or auditory stimulation? What does the room look like from a child's perspective?

What's the temperature like? Is there a draft or is the sun in your eyes? Can you wait outside?

Imagine yourself waiting in this room for one hour, two hours or longer? As you became more tired/bored/distressed/unwell how would the room meet you where you are? If the room could speak, what might it say?

Before you finish your scan, slowly look around the room and choose someone (without them being aware) and repeat quietly in your mind:

Just like me, this person is looking for relief from suffering. Just like me, this person gets tired and hungry. Just like me, this person has waited for things that never arrived. May you be well. May you be happy. May you be free from suffering.

## Conclusion

In this chapter, you've learned that you're able to exert some influence and control over your emotions by regulating your Drive, Threat and Soothe systems. You have also learned some new ways to breathe and move that will help build your compassionate nature.

This chapter is a reset. It's all about learning to do things differently. With some curiosity and playfulness, you can go on an adventure and learn new ways to bring your full awareness to the work of being a Compassion Revolutionary.

Practise the breathing exercises or the mindfulness meditation each day for five minutes for the next three weeks and you will begin to notice a difference. Every morning, when you have your first cup of coffee or tea, or glass of water and lemon, I'd like you to stop for a moment and simply taste that first sip. This is how we bring ourselves back into our body.

In the next chapter, you are taking everything you've learned so far and using it in service of yourself. Chapter Four is all about self-compassion. You know that critical voice that continually chatters away, comparing you to others and giving you unhelpful and anxiety provoking advice? I'm going to show you where the off switch is.

# 4

# Self-compassion

*You yourself, as much as anybody in the entire universe,
deserve your love and affection.*

*Sharon Salzberg*

## Introduction

Directing compassion towards yourself is not all that different to
directing compassion towards others. You know when you get on
a plane and the flight attendant does the safety drill? They will
say, 'Put on your own oxygen mask first' – that's self-compassion.
Or when you apply sunscreen before you spend time outdoors.
Keep these metaphors in mind as you read this chapter.

In Chapter Two, we learned about SUMA.

The very first step involved Showing Up so you can be aware
of what is happening. If you don't show up, you won't notice the
suffering and distress that is right there in your body. You won't notice
the joy and liberation either.

Step Two was all about Understanding and making sense of what's happening. You pass a homeless woman on the street. Is it cold outside? Are her blankets wet? Does she have shoes? You might decontextualise this distress as you ask yourself – why is it that so many women in my area are living without secure housing? What are the politics of housing supply and mental health services that are determining this housing crisis?

Then Step Three where you need to Move Closer so that your heart responds to her distress. The word compassion literally means 'to suffer with'. You will notice that you start to feel warmth and tenderness towards this woman. You don't make a judgement, as in that moment you understand that we could all be in her position. A collection of actions colliding might leave any of us vulnerable and unsupported. Or you might feel into the privilege and safety that you have been bestowed with and in that moment, open your heart wider to express deep gratitude.

Lastly, you act. Compassion helps you find a way to understand this person's distress. Maybe you say hello and smile, or you stop and talk or you tuck some money under her pillow or you buy her a coffee. Maybe you simply put your hands together as you pass and bow your head a little. This is part of the shared human experience.

Self-compassion is no different. It involves acting in the same way towards yourself when you're in distress, when you fail, when you make a mistake or when you drop the ball. Rather than ignoring your own distress, crossing the street to be away from yourself, or telling yourself to 'suck it up sweetheart,' you respond with compassion and acknowledge that things are difficult right now or that you're overwhelmed. You might have a fresh realisation that you are human and human beings are not able to be perfect – no matter how hard we try. That's the joy and the pain of the human experience.

Directing compassion towards ourselves is vital and because we often leave ourselves out in the cold, I am devoting this entire chapter to the practice of bringing compassion home to ourselves. Generally, we fear self-compassion, we label it a weakness and worry we will lose the race if we keep making these 'pit stops' to care for ourselves. As any formula one driver knows – no fuel, no race.

Criticising and reprimanding is not a great motivator. You may think you can beat yourself up to increase your productivity. This strategy will not work long-term. Continued criticism will cause you to freeze or become anxious. You are conditioning yourself to dread failure and mistakes. This fear inhibits action. You start to withdraw from your own wonderful self and stifle the emergence of compassion. Self-compassion is like learning a new language. You find a new vocabulary to speak to yourself with. Words that are wise and brave and loving.

Self-compassion is associated with positive psychological strengths, such as happiness, optimism, wisdom, curiosity, personal initiative and emotional intelligence.[1]

Another strength of being self-compassionate is it helps us deal with all the things that life throws at us: health problems; relationship break-ups; our experience of trauma; not getting the promotion. All the things that happen to all of us at one time or another and sometimes all at once. When you are compassionate towards yourself, you free yourself up to enjoy your relationships with others. Your empathic concern increases, you become more altruistic, and your perspective widens along with your tendency towards forgiveness. You might want to quit smoking or stick to a healthy eating plan or follow up on those medical tests. Self-compassion helps with all of this.

# What self-compassion is not

## Self-compassion is not self-pity

We tend to confuse self-compassion with a range of unhelpful behaviours. Self-compassion is not self-pity. Remember the last time you were absorbed with self-pity. Self-pity is a view of the world as hostile to our needs and wishes. We think 'why do I have to clean up this mess? Everyone else has the day off. I'm so unlucky'. Even as I write this, I can hear *Nobody Knows the Trouble I've Seen* playing in the distance. Self-pity erodes our sense of connection and interdependence.

## Self-compassion is not the same as self-esteem

When we aim for high self-esteem we are working on ensuring that others recognise and value our skills or our social position. I've worn my share of shoulder pads in the 90s, I've practised Amy Cuddy's Power Pose and I've tried leaning in like the COO of Facebook. This is not self-compassion. It's often just an inaccurate view that we try to convince ourselves and others to take seriously. Self-compassion sees through all of that and recognises that we are giving things our best shot and we are worth no more when the wheel of fortune stops at the jackpot than we are when we turn up at a meeting with a forgotten tea towel draped across our shoulder. (Am I the only one who has ever done this?) I'm inviting you to extend compassion towards yourself because all living creatures deserve unconditional compassion and understanding. Not because you look immaculate or you know some big words. Not because you were born into privilege or because you overcame enormous odds. But because you are so much more than enough.

## Self-compassion is not self-indulgence

I hear this all the time: if I practise self-compassion, I will let myself get away with everything. But self-compassion helps us do the things that are good for us.

On a chilly winter's morning, self-compassion encourages us to get up and get moving so we make it to our gym session. And when we roll over and go back to sleep, self-compassion will nod and remind you that tomorrow morning is another day. As we practise more acceptance and self-compassion we move closer to ourselves. We begin to open up to our own constructive feedback rather than shutting down to protect ourselves from insult and injury. Sometimes things don't go well. Sometimes we need to receive critical feedback about our performance. If we apply this nonjudgmental, accepting self-compassion towards ourselves, we're able to open up and hear that feedback. We can even reflect more clearly and openly about how we may improve our performance.

If we meet ourselves with judgement and harshness, ready to beat ourselves up, we're less likely to want to be fully honest – even with ourselves. We want to be able to hear constructive feedback. We want to be able to be self-reflexive. We want to be able to consider how we have performed and how we can improve on that. We can do this in a way that is compassionate. We are human beings, not human doings.

*A truce can be called in your inner war. Peace is possible. Your old habits of self-criticism don't need to rule you forever. What you need to do is listen to the voice that's already there, even if a bit hidden – your wise, compassionate self.*

*Dr Kristen Neff*

## Three elements of self-compassion

Self-compassion doesn't mean you're not accountable for your actions. It's not a free pass to behave without regard for yourself or for others. We can recognise where we have erred and be compassionate towards ourselves. I don't want to give you the impression that I am always acting with self-compassion. Just like the rest of humankind, I meet my edge and trip into self-pity or self-criticism. You will also come up against that edge, and each time you can nestle into the practice of compassion: Show up, Understand, Move Closer and Act.

Kristen Neff has identified three elements of self-compassion:[2]

- self-kindness vs. self-judgment
- common humanity vs. isolation
- mindfulness vs. overidentification.

When we practise self-compassion we aim to move away from self-criticism and self-judgment and stay with kindness. We remind ourselves that we are part of a larger humanity that also experiences distress and failure. We train towards staying with the present moment rather than become over-identified or absorbed with the distress. Let me use a story about my last vacation to help you see how this plays itself out.

In 2018, I was heading to Berlin for a much-needed holiday. My back was tense from a lot of leaning over my computer until late at night trying to get ahead of my work schedule so I could enjoy a work-free holiday. Just as I stepped off the plane on the Berlin tarmac, I pinched a nerve in my lower back. The compression caused a bolt of electric pain to shoot down my leg. Every slight move set it off again. It was the beginning of my holiday in a city I had dreamed about – and there I was, in excruciating pain, barely able to step onto the shuttle bus to collect my luggage. The pain was unrelenting.

For the next four days, I was unable to move outside my apartment. I'd travelled a long way to lie in a big bed, eating frozen yoghurt and watching Netflix, dosed high on pain relief. My mind went straight to self-judgement. I scolded my own body: why are you letting me down? You should have made a physio appointment before you left Australia, I berated myself. Surely, you knew this would happen and you should have taken steps to prevent it.

I slipped into self-pity. I felt I had failed in the art of holidays. I thought I had ruined my partner's holiday and I was saying to myself, 'what a loser you are.' The pain was unbearable at times and I couldn't sit for long. I had to be careful when turning at the hips to avoid further compression. In my mind I was the first and only person to embark on a holiday and be knocked out on Day One by nerve pain. I wanted to go home. I was tired and trapped. I had moved over to a sense of isolation rather than common humanity. All I thought about was the pain. I was trapped inside a story where I was the central character and I led the plot around in circles.

By Day Three I recognised what was happening and I started to shift my attention towards self-compassion. I reminded myself throughout the day that I deserved love and care because I'm a human being, not because things work out well. I wrote down in my notebook – may I accept this pain without thinking it makes me a failure.

I started to ask myself some helpful questions. 'What do you need right now, Mary? What would help? What feels the hardest right now?' In this way, I expressed self-kindness rather than self-judgement. I offered myself the things I needed: afternoon naps and delicious frozen yoghurt. I asked my partner if he would find me a walking stick. I started to accept his kindness and care without resentment. I stopped planning to make it to the Plaza 'tomorrow'. I stopped wishing I was somewhere else. I was leaving over-identification and leaning into a mindful acceptance. I watched through my window in the early evening as people drifted home from work. I noticed how the light changed throughout the day.

Here I was, in Berlin. I reminded myself that things change and nothing is fixed. I repeated to myself 'right now it's like this, but it won't always be like this'. Through my window, I noticed a beautiful older man in a smart Trilby hat. He walked past our apartment each day, stooped and shuffling. I imagined he was in great pain. Some days I would send him little silent wishes for goodness. One day I remember thinking to myself, I hope someone makes you a warm tea when you get to wherever you are going. In this way, I started to move closer to the idea of common humanity, instead of this isolation where I thought that I was the only person in Berlin who was in agony.

By Day Four I was able to move about, albeit very slowly with my trusty walking stick. I discovered my little street, Rosa-Luxemburg-Straße was quaint and beautiful. We often miss the small intricate details, the little things of beauty, in our haste to see the next thing. I was forced to slow down and concentrate on small things. There was an ice-cream shop near where I was staying that sold the most amazing flavours. People cued up in a long winding line that snaked down the street. The ice-cream maker was from Italy and he had a head of the wildest hair – like crazy fairy floss. One day I saw a small child so lost in her ice-cream – it made me smile.

There was a paper shop at the end of my street that sold the tiniest Japanese paper bags with the most exquisite designs on them. They are made for putting money in as a gift. I decided I would put a love note in them and give them to friends when I got home.

Being forced to move very, very slowly helped me become more mindful and less over- identified. Now my holiday felt like a little miniature adventure, and I started to feel warmer and more lighthearted. I looked forward to slow evening strolls with my partner as we investigated our neighbourhood. What I didn't know that day on the tarmac in Berlin was that it would be many months of physiotherapy before I'd be able to walk freely without the use of my trusty walking stick, but eventually I did fully recover.

## SUMA and self-compassion

SUMA works in exactly the same way when we direct compassion towards ourselves.

Step One: Show Up. I noticed how I needed to be with myself and noticed what was happening. I spent time being critical and harsh and feeling isolated until I showed up for myself. I noticed the way the unhelpful story was directing my thinking and my actions. I was able to say hello to my own misery.

Step Two: Understand. I started to see that this was a habitual pattern when I was overwhelmed or in great pain. I remembered times when I had felt a loss of control and my anxiety would escalate. Left unhindered it would gain speed, like a runaway trolley. I also started to understand that the long-haul flight from Australia to Berlin meant I had been seated for way too long in a warm cabin with little room to move. This exacerbated the likelihood that my muscles would cramp and dehydrate. All this led to a nerve compression. This wasn't just about me and my computer habit back home.

Step Three: Move Closer. Soon I started to accept the way things were and stop wishing I could be somewhere else. I gave myself reassurance and spoke to myself with kindness. I could be with myself and my frozen yoghurt and Netflix movies. I found life funny again.

Step Four: Act. There came a point where I started to practise connecting with the larger world and became less self-identified. I noticed the man with the Trilby hat and I sent him good wishes.

I asked my partner to find me a walking stick. I returned to my daily meditations.

Having exercises that you can turn to in times of pain is so helpful. For me it felt like I had a little kit of things I could experiment with to give myself love and care. The important thing for all of us to remember is that sometimes the pain doesn't go away and we don't give up. This is when we keep going. Keep returning to yourself. Saying hello over and over again to whatever arises. You are deserving of continued compassion.

# Self-compassion muscle workout

## Building our self-compassion muscle memory

Self-compassion requires active practice. It's not a theoretical exercise and it's no good just reading about it. In this section, you will discover some simple exercises that will help you move towards self-compassion. Each of these exercises will build your self-compassion repertoire and strengthen your self-compassion muscle. The more you practise, the more this will become your default position.

Over the years I have developed lots of simple ways to help me build self-compassion into my daily practice. I hope these ideas will help you just like they helped me in Berlin.

Pick one of these easy exercises and try it out when you're not feeling stressed or anxious. This will help you to prepare for when you need it.

### Self-compassion breaks

Set time aside where you focus on your own needs. Carve out 10 minutes each day when you turn off all the devices and take a break. In this moment you can breathe in and out and feel your feet planted on the floor. Time is no longer a bully. You can sit and greet yourself and notice what is happening in your own body. Hello, I am here, you say. 'Right now, it's like this, but it won't always be like this' is my favourite soothing reminder that nothing ever stays the same. Sometimes things end and sometimes they begin, sometimes they take a strange turning twist but right now, they are like this and we can be certain they won't always be this way.

## Music and art

Visit the places that bring you joy. Perhaps you love a certain piece of music or have a favourite place where you enjoy the art or the architecture or the graffiti. Play that music or visit that place and let yourself be absorbed in it. If you cannot physically visit the people and the places that bring you joy, you can visit them in your mind. While I have not been able to travel for the last 18 months because of quarantine restrictions I have travelled in my daydreams to a bakery in Sweden where I ate the largest sugary pretzel I have ever held in my hands. Using the wonder of the internet I have visited the Whitney Museum of American Art in New York and felt myself wandering through the Dawould Bey exhibition on the 8th floor.

We can also use music to remind ourselves to direct compassion towards ourselves. I was going through a particularly rough patch during a COVID-19 lockdown so I made myself a Spotify playlist, which included songs that made me feel uplifted and loved. Who would be on your playlist? Right now, I have the volume up on The Bengson's playing *My Joy is Heavy*.[3]

## Writing

Write yourself a love letter.[4] I often jot down a little note for myself and pin it to my computer or my bathroom mirror. Right now, I have a love note stuck to my mirror that says 'Love is my home'.

If you were to write yourself a note, what might it say?

### Treating yourself as a dear friend

When was the last time you bought yourself flowers? My friend Amy buys herself flowers at the end of each week. The ritual of coming home and arranging the flowers in a vase is her way of saying to herself, 'you are loved'.

Imagine writing a note to yourself from a dear loving friend. What would you say?

Dear Friend,

You are such an inspiration to me ...

### Soothing touch

Massage, being held and holding others is soothing. It relaxes us and activates our Soothing Drive. Our body releases oxytocin and we start to feel happier and calmer. You can gently stroke your own arms and face or fold your hands over each other or gently sway.

Using soothing touch is strongly supported by evidence. We can turn on our soothing system when we stroke our own skin, just as we are soothed when our skin is stroked by someone else – as long as it's the right person, like someone you feel close to or a massage therapist. As we stroke our own skin, we're soothing ourselves. Remember a time in your life when you have felt stressed. A time when you were the recipient of bad news and without even thinking, you might have started to stroke your own arms. This is our body responding and bringing us into a place of feeling more soothed.

### Food and water

Hydrate yourself, drink water and replenish yourself. You deserve it. You deserve to be hydrated.

Eat foods that bring you nourishment and energy. Eating the right amount is another form of self-care. Listen into your body and ask yourself, what do I need right now?

## Conclusion

In this chapter you've learned about self-compassion, how we take everything we've learned about compassion and we turn it towards ourselves. We've covered the things that self-compassion is not, and what it is. You now understand that there are three elements to self-compassion.

Now that you've got a handle on self-compassion, we're going to turn your attention to compassion for others. In the next chapter, you'll discover some of the barriers to acting with compassion towards others and how to recognise and respond to them. You'll also find out how to make your default position a compassionate one. Let's take everything we've learned so far and build on it.

# 5
# Compassion for others

*Small Kindness*
*I've been thinking about the way, when you walk*
*down a crowded aisle, people pull in their legs*
*to let you by. Or how strangers still say "bless you"*
*when someone sneezes, a leftover*
*from the Bubonic plague. "Don't die," we are saying.*
*And sometimes, when you spill lemons*
*from your grocery bag, someone else will help you*
*pick them up. Mostly, we don't want to harm each other.*
*We want to be handed our cup of coffee hot,*
*and to say thank you to the person handing it. To smile*
*at them and for them to smile back. For the waitress*
*to call us honey when she sets down the bowl of clam chowder,*
*and for the driver in the red pick-up truck to let us pass.*
*We have so little of each other, now. So far*
*from tribe and fire. Only these brief moments of exchange.*
*What if they are the true dwelling of the holy, these*
*fleeting temples we make together when we say, "Here,*
*have my seat," "Go ahead – you first," "I like your hat."*

*Danusha Lameris*[1]

# Introduction

In this chapter, we're going to turn our attention towards cultivating compassion for others. Right now, across the world, times are tough and the COVID pandemic and subsequent lockdowns and physical distancing measures are resurfacing old wounds and traumas. For many people, the pandemic has merely magnified the class, race and gender disadvantage they have navigated their whole lives. One thing is certain: we're all needing love and care right now, more than ever. We're also needing a powerful compassion to ensure we take what we are seeing and learning and use it to build a safer world.

In every moment there are so many invitations for us to offer compassion to this world that is full of suffering. The key to remaining buoyant and not burned out is learning the difference between abundant compassion and a type of pathological altruism that verges on martyrdom. I will explain these terms later in the chapter.

# Compassion is the antidote, not the poison

Compassion is often misunderstood as the cause of burnout and fatigue. We've even created a term for it – compassion fatigue. The term 'compassion fatigue' is a misnomer and I find it misleading and unhelpful. Let me explain why. People will often come to my Compassion Labs hoping I can give them some tips to avoid compassion fatigue. They will ask me to include this topic in the activities. I ask participants to list all the things that cause us fatigue at work. What are the things that are wearing you out? What are all the things that cause you exhaustion? Here's an abbreviated list I've compiled after years of holding space for people to answer this question.

- no access to fresh food and refreshments during my breaks, particularly on a night shift

- people being rude and dismissive
- the hours are so long
- my rostered hours are killing me
- sexism
- racism
- feeling unsafe physically and/or psychologically
- feeling unsupported by my boss or my organisation
- microaggressions that I deal with everyday
- electronic medical records
- electronic systems that don't talk to each other
- the unrelenting demand and the knowledge that I do not have the organisational resources to meet the need
- the sick feeling of dread when I am forced to work way beyond the point of exhaustion and I know something will go wrong.

So far I've never found anyone who includes 'compassion' as a thing that causes fatigue. No one has ever answered the question by saying, 'it's all the compassion I dish out, it's exhausting.'

It's the combination of an unsafe workplace; exposure to incivility, aggression and violence; insufficient resources to meet demand; technology, resources or a built environment that are not fit for purpose and the absence of a culture of care and respect. It's too easy to bundle all of these up and call them compassion fatigue.

One of the most overwhelming aspects of work in a caring or service delivery profession is moral suffering. Moral suffering occurs when you notice that there is distress and suffering and you determine a cause of action to bring about alleviation of the distress but are prevented from doing so because of an external or internal constraint.

This goes against your own moral sense of who you are and what you're here for. Moral injury is the wound or damage caused by transgressing your moral code. It is the pain, shame and distress that you experience as a result of participating in acts that are not part of your moral cartography. I've seen moral injury lead to overwhelming feelings of self-loathing, shame, loneliness and isolation. The practice of self-compassion becomes even more important to us during these times.

In Aged Care services I see staff who are exhausted and overwhelmed. They are often wedged between the physical demands of providing high quality care for older people and the insatiable demands from quality control bodies. The COVID-19 pandemic increased the vulnerability of aged care residents and the moral suffering of the workforce.

Empathic fatigue or overwhelm is different again. Empathic fatigue occurs when the expression of empathic emotion causes people to act in ways that don't reduce distress but in fact increase the likelihood of burnout. Empathic fatigue can be the result of pathological altruism, a form of altruism that harms ourselves and others when we continually work to help others until we are way beyond exhaustion, because we want to do good. Joan Halifax draws out the sometimes tangled relationship between our need to feel important or indispensable and our desire to alleviate distress.

> *... viewing ourselves as 'saving', 'fixing', and 'helping' others can feed our latent tendencies toward power, self-importance, narcissism and even deception of ourselves and others.*[2]

I've been there. I've been the one who jumped in to help when I didn't have the energy reserve or the available time to extend myself any further. This almost always results in me feeling resentful or unappreciated or just plain grumpy. When I notice these responses coming forward it's always a sign that I need to make friends with my ego and reassess my expectations of myself in my relationship with others.

This over-expectation, pushing, striving and demanding of ourselves is a form of what Thomas Merton refers to as 'contemporary violence'.

> *There is a pervasive form of contemporary violence to which the idealist most easily succumbs: activism and overwork. The rush and pressure of modern life are a form, perhaps the most common form, of its innate violence. To allow oneself to be carried away by a multitude of conflicting concerns, to surrender to too many demands, to commit oneself to too many projects, to want to help everyone in everything, is to succumb to violence. The frenzy of our activism neutralizes our work for peace. It destroys our own inner capacity for peace. It destroys the fruitfulness of our own work, because it kills the root of inner wisdom which makes work fruitful.*[3]

Empathic fatigue, moral injury and pathological altruism result in outcomes that are in complete opposition to the experience of abundant compassion.

This mistaken use of the term compassion fatigue has led many to believe that compassion is the poison. Compassion is actually the antidote. When we don't take the antidote, we remain frozen in place, fearful or anxious.

## Compassion in hard times

We all have stories of the infinite number of ways that we have been the recipient of compassion. The acts of sheer kindness and delight that have been directed towards us often by strangers.

I have both witnessed and been the recipient of so much compassion, both in small and exquisite gestures and in more robust and far-reaching efforts.

The start of 2019 in Australia saw the country ablaze. For those of you who live in other parts of the world, you most likely received the smoke, too. NASA reported that the plumes of smoke from the fires crossed South America, turning skies there hazy, and went on to make a full circuit around the globe. The devastation of these bushfires was immense. Seventy-five people lost their lives, 18 million hectares of land were burned and millions of animals were killed or injured.

In the midst of all the devastation there was an enormous outpouring of compassion. That's the thing that I love about life – when things are hard, we come together and love each other in new ways. People were serving their communities in so many ways. I remember being so touched by a story of a doctor who lost his clinic in the blaze and then started to see his traumatised patients in his motor home. There was the pharmacist who lost his home but stayed on in the community to help, knowing full well that so many would be without medication or prescriptions.

Then there were children in places far from Australia who were raising money through lemonade stands and Go Fund Me campaigns to give to our fire services. Women in the Netherlands were making mittens for the scorched paws of our koalas. Someone created an online service to connect those who were homeless with a spare bed. People began opening their homes to those who needed shelter. I was so incredibly moved by what I saw every day that I committed to drawing a small comic each day and posting it on an Instagram feed called My Year of Finding Beautiful.

At the time we had no idea that before the flames could possibly be extinguished, we would be plunged into a global pandemic. I know I took so much solace from Rebecca Solnit's book *Hope in the Dark*. I would turn over all the creased and worn-out pages – there have been so many times over the years when I have needed to hold fast to hope.

> *The world often seems divided between false hope and*
> *gratuitous despair. Despair demands less of us, it's more*
> *predictable, and in a sad way safer. Authentic hope requires*
> *clarity – seeing the trouble in this world – and imagination,*
> *seeing what might lie beyond these situations that are perhaps*
> *not inevitable and immutable.*[4]

Perhaps some of the most potent stories told about the power of compassion come from times of desperate human suffering and war. I am a loyal subscriber to the podcast *On Being* by Krista Tippett. As I write this chapter, I am thinking about her interview with Ariel Burger, an orthodox trained rabbi and author of *Witness: Lessons from Elie Wiesel's Classroom*. Ariel tells a story that he learnt from his son.[5]

It was the story of an older Jewish woman who was a prisoner of war in a Nazi concentration camp. One day the woman was transferred to a rabbit farm on the outskirts of Auschwitz. The Nazis were doing experiments on rabbits that had to do with finding a cure for typhus. This particular rabbit farm was run by a Polish man who noticed, pretty early on, that the rabbits were getting better quality food and attention and care than the Jewish slave laborers. So he started to sneak in food for the Jewish slave laborers and the inmates.

One day, the woman cut her arm on a piece of barbed wire, and the cut became infected. Of course, there was no way she was going to get antibiotics. The Polish man who was running the rabbit farm was moved to act with compassion and help this woman before her cut became seriously infected. So the man cut his own arm open, and he placed his wound on her wound so that he would get the infection that she had, and he became infected. He went to the Nazis, and he said, 'I'm one of your best managers. This rabbit farm is very productive. If I die, you're gonna lose a lot of productivity. I need medicine.' They gave him medicine, and he shared it with her. And he saved her life.

As Ariel Burger reflected on this story, he asked:

> *What does it take to be the kind of person who will share someone else's wound, in spite of all the pressure to see them as less valuable than a rabbit? What does it take to push against all that pressure and do the right thing, with courage and moral clarity, and to see another person as a person, when everything around you is telling you not to?*
>
> *And that question is the motivating question right now, because I think that's it not in those extreme situations alone, but in everyday life, how can we turn to the treasures of all of our human traditions, literatures, practices, to become better at that work? Because that, to me, is the most important thing. That's the root cause of all the other challenges and all the questions we're facing.*[6]

That is the question that we put to ourselves in this chapter. This is the fundamental question at the heart of a Compassion Revolution. The trick is not to think that the 'doing' is grand and far beyond us. To compare ourselves to others and imagine that whatever they are made of, however they arrange their lives, or whatever resources they have access to could not possibly mirror our lives.

My approach to compassion has always been to elevate the small and miraculous. I marvel at the way people care for one another. Our capacity for love and friendship and care is extraordinary. With this capacity comes responsibility. The responsibility we have for compassion is in the way we move through the world with an intention to bring love with us.

I recall a story told by Sensei Koshin Paley Ellison, a Zen teacher living in New York. He was leaving the New York Zen Centre, where he is President, and the doorman at his building said to him, 'I'm so curious about you. I've been watching you enter and leave this building for years. You and the other man who wears all black [his zen robes were black]. There's something about the way you walk down the street that makes me feel so good.' Ellison was surprised and said, 'Wow! Just the way I walk down the street?' The doorman nodded and said, 'Yeah, I don't know, but it makes me feel so good'.

Then Ellison went on to reflect that how we function is how we transform the culture of care. We do it in the most ordinary ways. The most pedestrian, simple, mundane and beautiful ways. How do we do this? We participate fully. We Show Up. We drop into our bodies and widen out. The courage is that we do it again and again, knowing full well we won't get it perfect. But we make a commitment to take responsibility for showing up and loving where we are and loving what we are doing and loving who we are doing it with.

# Compassion muscle workout

### The practices

Compassion isn't an intellectual exercise, it is an embedded practice. Just as you don't form muscle mass by thinking and reading about the idea of improving your core strength, you don't practise compassion by reading about it. In so many ways, this chapter is all about developing your core strength. We are not practising doing good, being perfect or improving ourselves or being a better person. No, we are practising SUMA. And it starts with showing up and it ends with action. There are important exercises that we can do to train our minds to pay attention and to train our hearts to remain soft. These practices give us the supportive foundation for compassionate actions.

In this section I am going to step you through three practices that you can dip in and out of. Each of these practices has been audio recorded on the Compassion Revolution Care website if you prefer an audio instruction – visit www.compassionrevolution.care

All of these meditations will lead towards your happiness.

## Loving-kindness or metta meditation

Loving-kindness meditation or metta meditation is an ultimate form of generous and selfless love towards ourselves and others. We commence this meditation with our heart centred on someone close to us who we find easy to love and slowly we move our attention out to a larger world. Metta is also a meditation where we send loving wishes to ourselves. We express our own deep desire to be free from the suffering and fear that keeps us stuck and because we are all in this together, we recognise that this fear keeps others stuck too and we send them wishes to be free.

1. Gently close your eyes if you feel comfortable doing that, or direct your eyes towards the floor while seated or lying down.
2. Begin with a few deep breaths. Check in with where you're starting this moment from – physically, emotionally, mentally.
3. Consider a person in your life who is easy to care about. This could be a good friend, a partner, perhaps an animal. Imagine them sitting in front of you and looking into your eyes.

4.  Get a sense of your heart in this moment, and with intention say to this person, 'May you be happy. May you be healthy in body and mind. May you be safe and protected from inner and outer harm. May you be free from fear, the fear that keeps you stuck.'

5.  Again, breathing in and breathing out, reconnect with your heart.

6.  Now incline your heart and mind towards yourself and say to yourself, 'May I be happy. May I be healthy in body and mind. May I be safe and protected from inner and outer harm. May I be free from fear, the fear that keeps me stuck.'

7.  And now breathing in and breathing out, consider a person in your life you don't know too well. Perhaps the check-out person at your local market, or someone at work you've never spoken to.

8.  Connecting with your heart once again, and just like you did for the person who's close to you, say now to them: 'May you be happy. May you be healthy in body and mind. May you be safe and protected from inner and outer harm. May you be free from fear, the fear that keeps you stuck.'

9.  And breathing in and out, now bringing to mind someone in your life who you've had difficulty with. Someone you're frustrated, irritated or annoyed with.

10. And imagine them sitting here, looking into your eyes and with the same intention and heartfulness that you had for the person who it was easy to care for, now say to them: 'May you be happy. May you be healthy in body and mind. May you be safe and protected from inner and outer harm. May you be free from fear, the fear that keeps you stuck.'

11. And now imagine expanding this sense of heartfulness and intention throughout the entire world. All countries, all people.
12. Saying to them: 'May you be happy. May you be healthy in body and mind. May you be safe and protected from inner and outer harm. May you be free from fear, the fear that keeps you stuck.'
13. And breathing in and breathing out, as we end this practice gently do another mindful check-in. Get a sense of how you're feeling now, without any judgments. What emotions are present? Is your mind busy or calm?
14. Perhaps end by thanking yourself, and all the people who you included in this practice.
15. And when you're ready, gently open your eyes.

You might be thinking that you can't 'do' meditation well enough, or that you've tried it in the past and it didn't work. Maybe your mind wanders, or you fall asleep while you're meditating. That's completely okay. You're absolutely right – meditation is not everyone's jam. If you've experienced trauma you may find it hard to close your eyes and sit still. I often have people in Compassion Labs whose eyes will not shut, instead they flutter endlessly. You may find that lying down and listening to the recorded version of these practices feel safer and more helpful.

You can find the recording on the Compassion Revolution website.[7]

## Just like me

I use *Just Like Me Meditation* all the time. It's been my go-to during the COVID-19 pandemic, when lots of us were feeling anxious and grumpy. I found it so helpful to remember that, essentially, we're all seeking happiness in our lives and we're all trying to avoid suffering. During strict lockdown, when my allotted time at the supermarket would come, every second day, there would be lots of anxious people trying to outstrip the supply of toilet paper. As I looked at that person who somehow needed 40 rolls of toilet paper, I would remind myself that 'Just like me, this person is seeking to fill their needs.' Sometimes, when I couldn't remember all of the words in this meditation, I would have my little shorthand, which was 'Just like me, this person is learning about COVID.' I felt we weren't so far away from each other. I didn't need as much toilet paper, but essentially we were both fearful and trying to look after ourselves in what was a tricky time.

## Just Like Me exercise

(Adapted from the meditation of Ram Das.)

This exercise can be done anywhere that people gather (supermarkets, business meetings, zoom calls, staff meetings, parks and airports).

In Compassion Labs, I ask participants to choose someone in the room (without that person knowing you have chosen them) then we quietly go through these five steps, repeating them silently inside our heads. When we are finished, we move on.

> With attention on the person, repeat to yourself silently:
> Just like me, this person is seeking some happiness in their life.
> With attention on the person, repeat to yourself silently:
> Just like me, this person has known sadness, loneliness and despair.
> With attention on the person, repeat to yourself silently:
> Just like me, this person is seeking to fulfill their needs.
> With attention on the person, repeat to yourself silently:
> Just like me, this person is learning about life.

# Gratitude

*If the only prayer you ever said was thank you, that would suffice.*

*Meister Eckhart*

Gratitude is super powerful. It motivates others, brings appreciation into the room and improves our health both psychologically and physically. Gratitude simply recognises that the goodness we are experiencing is often due to the actions of another person. When we are grateful, we recognise the intention and effort that other people have invested in their actions that have contributed to our happiness. From the most mundane: when you bite into an apple you remember that someone grew that apple and others rose early in the day and stood in the cold air to pick that very apple. Someone else boxed the apple and another person collected it from the market or storehouse and placed it on the shelf at the grocery store. I'm grateful to that chain of human endeavour for bringing me a single red, sweet and juicy Royal Gala apple.

Other moments of gratitude have their antecedence in the decisions or the endurance of our ancestors. I find offering gratitude to those who came before me and will come after me to be a really grounding practice. To all the women who marched for freedom, who chained themselves to the gates of parliament, subjected themselves to the ridicule of men and kept standing up until they secured the vote and the right to sit in parliament, I offer gratitude.

When I first started to record the three things I was grateful for, I started out wide but it didn't take too long before I had started to notice the smallest things and feel so much thanks rising up. When I look back over my early Gratitude Journals, I have an entry that says: I'm so grateful for my soft woolly jumper in the cold today. I needed you and you were right there!

Happiness sends signals to your central nervous system that you are safe and ready to feel more peaceful, less reactive, and less resistant. And it turns out that gratitude is the most effective practice for stimulating feelings of happiness. People who practise gratitude feel happier, and happier people are more satisfied with their lives, more resilient to stress and get along better with others. Grateful people are less depressed, achieve more and they are more helpful and generous.

In a study on gratitude, conducted by Robert A. Emmons, Ph.D., at the University of California at Davis and his colleague Mike McCullough at the University of Miami, randomly assigned participants were given one of three tasks.[8] Each week, participants kept a short journal. One group briefly described five things they were grateful for that had occurred in the past week, another five recorded daily hassles from the previous week that displeased them, and the neutral group was asked to list five events or circumstances that affected them, but they were not told whether to focus on the positive or on the negative. Ten weeks later, participants in the gratitude group felt better about their lives as a whole and were a full 25 per cent happier than the hassled group. They reported fewer health complaints, and exercised an average of 1.5 hours more.

## Gratitude – 14 Day Challenge

You don't need a special fancy journal, you simply need a notebook and pen.

Keep it by your bed or on your desk – somewhere that you will see it first thing each day or last thing each night.

Each day you write:

1.  I'm grateful for ....
2.  I'm grateful for ...
3.  I'm grateful for ...

Don't stress over it – jot three things down. The magic isn't making the three things poetic or perfect or grand. The magic lies in simply writing them down. At first it might seem awkward or even perfunctory. But over time, you will start to see the benefits. I promise.

## Good Finding – 7-day challenge

Practising gratitude in real time is a great way to encourage others and boost your own mood.

Let's go Good Finding, searching out people who are doing great stuff and letting them know I see what they're up to! This is one of my favourite ways to live.

Here's the challenge for you. I want you to find three people every day and let them know you appreciate them. You will find people who are surprised that you have seen them. That night they will travel home to their families and spread joy because gratitude, happiness and encouragement is contagious. Hearing 'thank you' from your boss boosts self-worth and self-efficacy, and we all want to be boosting some of that.

When I actively practise Good Finding I start to see people doing beautiful things. I told my postman last week that I loved the way he smiled so wide every time he brought my mail to my door. I will often send a message to a writer to let them know how much I appreciated their book. I write to say, 'I see you, over there tapping away to bring these words to me and I love you for it'. I live opposite a small park and I get so many opportunities to tell parents that they are doing a sterling job of raising the next generation. The generation that will likely support me in my old age.

This is the currency that keeps our world humming along.

**So here's my invitation:**

Over the next seven days, I'm inviting you to go Good Finding for three people each day.

Just three people every day. Post your results on socials using this hashtag –#GoodFindingChallenge so we can keep the whole thing going.

## Conclusion

In the next chapter, we're going to look at how to take compassion to work. We spend an enormous amount of time at work, investing our energy and our intellect. This is time spent away from our families and our friends, our hobbies and much of the things that give us pleasure. Imagine if our place of work was compassionate and kind. It could be.

# 6

# Taking compassion
# to work

*We see horrible things, we have to put them away when we
go home to our families. One day we will run out of hiding
places.*

@GongGasGirl (Twitter)

The current system of healthcare we have built up over the last
150 years, from the commencement of the second industrial
revolution, is toppling over. It is staggering and bloated, weighed
down by the damage done by fast food industries, sedentary
lifestyle, economic and racial inequality and every smart
technological advancement that lengthens our lifespan. We are
bed-blocked and whipped by metrics. On top of all this, we are now
in the grip of a global pandemic. Jobs have been lost in hospitality,
tourism and the arts and across Australia many of us are in strict
lockdown. It's been a tough couple of years.

## What's happening at work?

In October 2018 the College of Intensive Care Medicine (CICM) revoked the Intensive Care Unit's training accreditation at a Sydney Hospital after allegations of bullying by senior medical staff.[1] In effect this means that the CICM were not confident of the hospital's ability to provide an adequate and safe teaching environment for CICM trainee doctors.

In 2017 the *Sydney Morning Herald* ran a story about the experience of depression among doctors and highlighted the sense of impending doom and escalating panic that is often felt by doctors in training as they complete ward rounds.[2]

> *Any minute now, she realised, the spotlight would turn on her, and she would be asked for her professional opinion. Introverted and shy by nature, she was gripped by a wave of performance anxiety. There were some consultants, she had discovered, who could sniff out her fear and make a meal of it. The process of annihilation had begun.*
>
> *Kathy Evans*[3]

In the 2017 AMA (Australian Medical Association) in NSW survey (conducted after the tragic spate of suicides by young doctors), more than two-thirds of junior doctors in NSW said they feared for their own health and safety owing to overwork, and 71 per cent were anxious about making clinical errors because of fatigue.

One of the most shared Instagram posts from Humans of New York is a photo of a medical resident who said, "On the first day of rotations, my attending physician told me: 'I'm an asshole, but I'll make you a better doctor.' He made fun of me in front of other students. He put me down in front of patients. He'd threaten to kick me out every day … after going through hell, I just don't care anymore."[4]

If we need any further alarm bells to sound: a study in the *European Heart Journal* in 2019 reveals that those people who are exposed to bullying and violence are at higher risk of cardiovascular disease.[5]

Becoming a doctor can prove fatal. In a study sponsored by the American College of Surgeons, 6 per cent of respondents considered suicide and there was a strong correlation with burnout.[6] In the United States, suicide is estimated to be the second leading cause of death among medical residents, after cancer (by contrast, the leading cause of death in the general population for that age group – 25 to 40 – is trauma.) Suicide statistics for young doctors are difficult to track because many deaths are not reported as suicide. But we know that at least one doctor completes suicide every day in the United States.

Vets are about four times as likely to take their own life than the general Australian population and twice as likely as healthcare workers. One vet will die by suicide every 12 weeks, figures from the Australian Veterinary Association show.[7] When I take my Tenterfield Terrier to the vet, it looks like a fairly easy job with patients who can't talk back. But vets care for animals that are not accidentally injured and are often subject to abuse from the animal's owner. They provide complex and important critical care for animals. During the catastrophic bushfires across Australia many rural vets spent their days humanely euthanising farm animals. This took an enormous toll on their mental wellbeing.

In a recent study of Australian surgeons, 47 per cent of surgeons (both trainees and practising surgeons) reported being a victim of bullying and 68 per cent reported witnessing bullying.[8] A US Workplace Bullying Survey conducted by the Workplace Bullying Institute in 2007 reported that 49 per cent of workers are victims of or witness to bullying and a significant number of victims suffer post-traumatic stress disorder. The sad truth is that we would likely find bullying is endemic if we looked carefully enough.

Bullying and violence are common in healthcare workplaces and studies have shown that those exposed to these stressors are at higher risk of cardiovascular disease. The Royal Australasian College of Surgeons reports on their website, 'Bullying is a real problem for our profession, like it is in the rest of the health sector. It compromises patient safety. Almost half of us have seen it or felt it. Now is the time to build respect and improve patient safety in surgery and deal with discrimination, bullying and sexual harassment.'

Trainee doctors and nurses speak to me about falling asleep at the wheel of their cars after long night shifts. Many of them have crashed their cars. In a workshop I held with emergency nurses, a participant spoke to the room about how her aunt, also a nurse, died in a car accident driving home from a night shift. The room became silent. Then after a few minutes of quiet tension, a younger nurse cleared her throat and said, 'We always joke about this stuff, we say "seeya, hope you don't fall asleep on the way home" or we drink so much coffee and talk about feeling like a zombie. But today this feels really serious, it doesn't seem funny anymore.'

These stories speak to a crisis in our modern healthcare system. This crisis has gripped the industrialised world of medicine. We are damaging the very people who we rely on to help us when we need to be cared for. We have created a sick-care system, not a healthcare system.

In a first global analysis of the loss of life and health associated with working long hours, WHO and ILO (International Labour Organization) estimated that, in 2016, 398 000 people died from stroke and 347 000 from heart disease as a result of having worked at least 55 hours a week.[9] Between 2000 and 2016, the number of deaths from heart disease due to working long hours increased by 42 per cent, and from stroke by 19 per cent.

Overall, the study – drawing on data from 194 countries – said that working 55 hours or more a week was associated with a 35 per

cent higher risk of stroke and a 17 per cent higher risk of
dying from ischemic heart disease compared with a 35–40 hour
working week.

The study covered the period 2000–2016, and so did not include
the COVID-19 pandemic. Some workers have shown a 9 per cent
increase in hours worked during the pandemic.

It doesn't have to be like this. Workplaces can be fertile grounds
for compassion. Our interactions can soothe, calm, and increase
happiness. This requires relational and interpersonal work. This work
of caring for one another is the very glue that enables organisations
to function safely and productively. I see great examples in healthcare
of people who are connected to their purpose so strongly that it plays
itself out every day at work. They are able to be with others *and* take
care of themselves. Writer Annie Dillard famously said, 'How we
spend our days is, of course, how we spend our lives.' For many of us,
a large portion of our days is spent at work; in fact, the average person
will spend 90,000 hours at work over a lifetime. We need to invest
that time compassionately.

It's the breathing, moving, fearful, joyful, hungry, tired or
exuberant human being that comes to work every day. We work
with real people. Our colleagues have tossed and turned at night,
physically caught trams and trains and buses to get to be with us,
they've kissed goodbye the wet faces of small children and hunted
for lost keys. They are not flesh-covered thinking machines. We
get tired and we get sick. We worry. And then we get up and go
to work.

At night you travel home from work in the darkened tram.
You've been shouted at by your manager or ignored by a colleague or
come to the realisation that you are not going to be promoted. You
absentmindedly wonder if your small business is going to survive the
major corporate takeovers. Maybe you've held the hand of a patient

as they sucked their last breath or maybe today was an exceptionally good day and you're humming *Don't Worry, Be Happy*. Work travels with us. We take it home, where no one, except us, will befriend it. The Centre for Grief Recovery estimated that the hidden cost of workplace grief exceeds $75 million per year.[10]

There are real and devastating consequences of the rising rate of health professional stress, fatigue, depression, anxiety and burnout. These consequences impact at an individual level, they are damaging to the healthcare system and dangerous for patients.

Research has shown that task errors by emergency doctors are an outcome of interruptions, multitasking and fatigue. In other words: when doctors are exhausted and required to complete multiple tasks, all at the same time, they make mistakes. No surprise there. Doctors are also 15 times more likely to make prescribing errors when they are sleep-deprived.

For so long we have imagined that this is the system we have and the best we can hope for are modifications and concessions. During the COVID-19 pandemic, frontline workers were fighting for adequate Personal Protective Equipment and celebrating when they finally got fit-tested for a decent mask. In so many places this was a hard-won battle and in many other places the war to protect their respiratory system has not been won. Across Victoria and New South Wales, the population is currently in lockdown and schools are closed. Re-opening schools is now dependent on ventilation assessments, carbon dioxide monitors and particle filters. It seems startling that we are only now taking ventilation and clean air seriously in schools. These gains were not granted without pressure and demands. This is the muscular nature of compassion. We see a larger world is possible and we roll up our sleeves and bang our hands on the table. We remind ourselves of the feminist rallying cry from 2017 'nevertheless she persisted' and we keep going.

# Re-imagining compassion at work

Grace Lee Boggs was a Chinese-American philosopher, civil rights legend and social visionary. She believed that we can be aware that we cannot continue to live and work in the same way but at the same time we feel immobilised because we cannot imagine an alternative. You know that feeling of immobilisation. It is both alarming and dispiriting.

Grace Lee Boggs held to the view that our way of being in the world and indeed the world we are 'being in' is not fixed or immutable.[11] But rather than turning our back on 'the twisted shape of things', we need to own the way things are so that we can imagine our way forward into something far more life-giving and sustainable.

> *The opportunity that we now have to reimagine everything,*
> *to reimagine work – to think of it as productive not only*
> *of things, but of well-being – to think of governance in*
> *a different way, to think of education in a different way.*
> *What an opportunity. What a time to be alive. We're not*
> *only being, but we're non-being and becoming.*[12]

This is what we must do as Compassion Revolutionaries; resist and create new ways of relating to each other at work. These new ways of relating will seem small but they are not insignificant. Everything that we do to resist the pull of the economic systems towards a care-less economy is something and it is something very powerful. Every time we diverge from the taken for granted way of being in the workforce and enact more compassion, it is an act of mighty resistance. This is what it means to be a revolutionary. This is what it means to be compassionate.

When we keep compassion at the very centre of our practice, we become more resilient to stress and immune to burnout and we find our work more inspiring. When our organisations practise a culture of compassion we see a reduction in employee exhaustion and sick leave. These organisations will have a higher level of positive emotion for their staff. Put simply: compassionate organisations care for their people. The economic and moral return on this investment is significant.

Great change does not happen like a 'shot out of a pistol'. This revolution of compassion will not happen because of an overthrow. It will happen because of a transition. This is how new epochs arrive. When Grace Lee Boggs was 99 years old, in 2015, she declared that we were in an 'epoch transition'. This is that transition. But first we have to own the system, knowing that we created it and now it is broken, and we must build something new in its place. What will we build?

## Compassionate leadership

On Friday 15th March 2019, we heard the news that a right-wing extremist had attacked two separate mosques in Christchurch, New Zealand. Fifty-one people were killed and many more were injured. I'm not going to write about the terror, the brutality and the horror of that attack. At the time, I remember feeling caught up in a thick weight of emotions and a deeper recognition of the extent of Islamaphobic hate crimes. I recognised that I wasn't alone.

The whole world watched the New Zealand Prime Minister, Jacinda Ardern, as she stepped up and showed us what Compassionate Leadership looks like. Her response to this crisis was so generative, so brave and fearless and all at once full of tenderness. At the time I was writing an essay on Compassionate Leadership (that would later form the core of this chapter) and at the same time, watching a woman role model these attributes on the global stage.

*One of the criticisms I've faced over the years is that I'm not aggressive or assertive enough … or maybe because I'm empathetic I'm weak. I totally rebel against that. I refuse to believe that you cannot be compassionate and strong.*[13]

This extreme act of terror gave rise to a wave of compassion that has served to instruct me on the strength and tenacity that compassion brings. In her evening press conference, just hours after the terrorist attack, Prime Minister Ardern looked sombre and calm, her dark hair pulled back from her tired face. She spoke with clarity and conviction, taking great effort to give as much information as she had to hand. She detailed what had occurred, how many men were in custody and what little the New Zealand police knew about them at that stage. She updated the world on how many had died and how many were injured and where they were receiving medical care. She went on to give assurance about the presence of heightened security and the importance of keeping people safe.

Then she addressed those who had been impacted by the acts of violence. She reminded us that these people might not have been born in New Zealand but that they had come here and this was their home and they were loved. This is not a small point. This was the first time we had heard a Western leader speak about people of the Muslim faith as worthy and deserving of our love. In her press conference she coined the now famous hashtag #TheyAreUs. These people were not 'other', they were 'us'.

*Many of those who will have been directly affected by this shooting may be migrants to New Zealand, they may even be refugees here. They have chosen to make New Zealand their home, and it is their home. **They are us.** The person who has perpetuated this violence against us is not.*[14]

She hugged Muslim men, just as she did women, with a comfort that betrayed no self-consciousness. The power of her response came not only from her warm physical embrace of the survivors and families of victims, but also from symbolic gestures such as wearing the hijab and refusing to use the name of the chief suspect. This was backed up with the right messaging and followed swiftly with practical measures, such as new gun legislation.

One of the questions that is regularly asked of me by leaders is: How can we balance compassion and accountability? It's like the corner of a well-worn rug that we keep tripping over. How can we lead with compassion and make sure that people still deliver the work; take responsibility for their actions; and come to work on time? In essence, how can I make sure that nothing bad happens on my watch and I don't get taken advantage of if I don't lead with some aggression?

That's the fear, isn't it? We want to be Jacinda Ardern but then we worry; how will all the work get done? Here's the thing: Jacinda Ardern wore a hijab and wrapped her arms around the grieving but she also determined to change gun legislation in New Zealand in just 72 hours. The work got done. It's not either/or.

I am inviting you to step up as leaders. We need a new paradigm shift away from a model of the organisation as a machine with leaders who are focused on ensuring the machine never stops. The old line-of-sight management, coupled with rigorous controls, strict policies, coercive punishment and lots of extrinsic rewards is over. Stop bribing people to do the great work they came into your organisation to do in the first place. Your staff do not want a cup-cake, they want your trust. They don't want to prove to you that they turned up on time, they want to do great work. And they want to do that work in a climate of trust and respect.

We work in complex-adaptive systems that breathe and give life to ideas and relationships. Our job as leaders is to enable the ecology of our organisation to grow human connection. I want us to start to think of these ecologies as verdant rather than arid. All the compassionate acts that we curate as leaders are part of what keeps our ecology lush with possibility and innovation and keeps our workforce well.[15, 16]

We only have to look at the effort and commitment that our workforce delivered throughout the COVID-19 pandemic. Suddenly leaders had to adapt to managing without direct line of sight. For many leaders this was difficult.

There is rigorous evidence that staff satisfaction is directly related to subsequent patient satisfaction.[17] When staff report that their line managers are supportive and their workplace is characterised by positive communication and staff involvement and they are able to deliver great patient care, this will directly predict patient satisfaction. Let's put that more simply; when staff believe they are being managed with compassion, lives will be saved. Where staff report a greater likelihood to leave their jobs, then patient satisfaction will be lower. Organisations that have a strong climate of trust and optimism do better for patients. These organisations also do better financially.

One of the highest predictors of patient mortality rates (in NHS Trusts) is the percentage of staff who are working in well-organised teams. The work of Michael West and his colleagues has been so instructive here.[18] These are people who know what team they belong to; what their role is, the contribution they are expected to make and with whom. These well-organised teams meet together regularly to exchange ideas, to review their performance and to support and encourage each other. These teams are effective, strong and vibrant. It makes such sense. And yet, again and again I interview staff who are unsure about their leader's expectations of them, or the expectations are so low they are not challenging or there are so many expectations they have no idea which one is the priority. Staff speak to me about not being allocated to a team or being allocated across so many teams they have no home base. Often I meet with staff who feel undermined by their manager and disconnected from their teams. This is not a matter of 'everyone playing nicely' – this is the very stuff that determines patient mortality.

Where we get this right, staff feel highly connected to their team. Staff commit to reviewing and shaping their individual and team objectives. The value and the importance for accountability and high-quality patient care is collectively reinforced. These teams are made up of people who are working effectively together and poor behaviour is addressed in real time and everyone is welcome to contribute to improvement. In these flourishing, verdant landscapes we see:

- lower levels of stress
- staff recommend these healthcare organisations as a place they would refer their friends and family
- staff experience overall better health: emotional, physical and psychological
- staff are less likely to present to work when they are unwell.

Let's look at the four steps of SUMA and see how this plays itself out in a complex acute setting.

1. Show Up: The leader takes care of themselves so they are able to manage their emotions and pay attention to their distress and the distress of others. They understand and are aligned with the values of the organisation and deeply care for their team and want to see them flourish and perform well.
2. Understand: The leader is open to listening to staff. They make sure staff understand that they are supported and they don't see

compassion as the 'soft stuff'. Maybe a team member confides to them that they feel they are the only one who is not making the grade. The team member is self-critical of their confidence and ability to stay the distance. After more listening the leader starts to see a pattern of distress. They begin to reflect on the local and systemic ways that they might influence the trend they are seeing.

3.  Move Closer: The leader remembers what it was like for them when they provided more clinical hours and in some ways they long for a return to some parts of that previous role. They recall that awful spiral of losing their confidence under the weight of all the unfinished discharge summaries and administrative tasks. They remember a tight knot that would often rise up their chest. 'How can I help?' they ask their staff.

4.  Act: The leader steps forward and together with their team they make a plan for providing each other with more care and attention. They brainstorm the ways that they might look out for each other. They decide to audit the eco-system of their department. They look at all the components of their work environment that impact on wellbeing:

    - the quality of the food and refreshments available for staff working overnight
    - the real and perceived safety of the team
    - the opportunities for connection
    - the system for receiving and giving feedback (both positive and negative)
    - how the team connects
    - how the team celebrates and grieves
    - the hours worked.

There are endless ways that we might overlay a SUMA lens on our leadership responsibilities. This is one simple example.

## Start now, use what you have

Interns can be revolutionaries, just as registrars can and consultants and directors of nursing and enrolled nurses and chief medical officers. Event managers, tailors, bakers, baristas, lawyers, pay-roll officers, cleaners and CEOs are all needed in this revolution.

At the conclusion of the very first Compassion Lab, which was held as a two-day retreat, we created a Compassion Manifesto. The Manifesto is available to download as a colour PDF poster at https://compassionrevolution.care/about-the-movement. This Manifesto includes the things that will make us well again framed with a deep, respectful recognition that there is much at stake.

## Compassion Revolution Manifesto

Say hello to Right Now.
Slow it right down so space can emerge.
We find opportunity for forgiveness, kindness, love.
Busy is the ~~new~~ old black.
There is power in the pause …
From mind-fullness to mindfulness.
Sit still. Stop what you are doing.
B R E A T H E and L I S T E N
Speak up loud for listening.
Really listening.
Our mind and body can work together to calm us.
Big exhalations slow our heart rate.
Compassion isn't the soft stuff. Compassion is muscular.
To be courageously compassionate takes tenacity and strength.
There is a violence to overwork and over-promising to the
   demands of work.

Self-compassion refuses this invitation.

Choose to be your own best friend.

Say hello to time ... alone.

Right now it's like this. It won't always be like this.

Compassion empowers people.

We awaken compassion as we grow empathy and practice mindfulness.

Find your tribe and love them.

When we spend time with people in a shared space, we start to hum with them in dynamic resonance.

We are human. We like to look into each other's eyes and feel each other's touch.

Give up the idea that you can multi-task.

Stretch on a yoga mat.

Eat mindfully. Laugh plentifully.

Do the things that scare you. Don't just talk about the things that scare you.

Vulnerability is a doorway to open-heartedness.

Open that door.

Welcome to Compassion Revolution.


I often think about the Tennessee Williams quote:

> *This world is a perpetually burning building and what we must rescue from it, every time is love.*

Our health and social care system is a burning building too. What we must rescue from it, every single time, is love.

This is how we count the right things. This is how we define the contours of compassion as an act of mighty resistance.

We don't need any magic powers to see that our health and social care systems are in need of help and that the way forward is going to take a lot of hard work and the solution is not 'soft'. I frequently work with services that are broken. The whole system no longer works in a way that is functioning and often organisations start to operate like one big sprawling family at Christmas. All the cousins have turned up with their kids and grandma has left her hearing aid at home. Half the family don't speak to each other and every Christmas it seems like your sister has a new husband. It gets ugly and someone bursts into tears and doors slam. The turkey is bigger than the oven, everyone has overspent on their credit card and resentment is brewing. You know the drill. We've all been there.

These organisations are filled with highly qualified and highly skilled clinicians, doing exceptional work often to the point of exhaustion.

This is what a broken system looks like. Unfortunately, this is not unique to this hospital. We have seen this before and we will see this again. This is the environment where I frequently deliver compassion training. These are the leaders who refer to compassion as the 'soft stuff'. This is the system where compassion is so desperately needed.

But the good news is that everyone within an organisation can make small steps that begin to make a significant difference. Now is the time to find other people within your organisation who you can pair up with to make a difference. There is so much power in working with others who are keen to make the world a better place. Start a Compassion Collaborative[19] to bring people across your organisation who share the same values and desire to make work a more powerfully compassionate place.

# Organisational compassion muscle workout

## Simple and genuine workout tips

Here are some of my favorite workouts that are simple and genuine:

- Greet everyone as you make your way to your desk or your department. A smile or a wave makes a big difference.
- If you're working from home you might like to arrange a morning check in via Zoom or a Slack group where everyone can post their morning emoji.
- Ask a colleague how they are doing. Don't forget to wait for the answer.
- Learn a bit about your co-worker's life. Ask people what land is home to them. Have genuine conversations about family members or what they did on the weekend. It is a delight when someone remembers your child's name or that you play netball.
- Do a coffee-run or make a pot of tea.
- Organise team days where your team can come together and give back to the community. Planting trees or cooking soup is an excellent way to come together in service of others.
- Start a Listening Circle or a Journal Reading Club. Making time to grow and reflect together builds trust.

Showing people you care, and creating policies that foster compassion, are simple but effective ways to improve business and care for each other. Our challenge is no longer to find a reason why compassion matters for business, instead it is time to design work and workplaces that foster compassion for everyone.

## Conclusion

In this chapter we have put the spotlight on organisations where things are not working so well and looked at some of the ways disrespect creates harm. You have also learned that we can all be architects of compassionate work. Even at a high level, you may feel an inertia and a learned helplessness.

Now that you've got a handle on creating a better organisational culture, we're going to turn our attention to creating a more compassionate world, one transformational step at a time.

# 7

# Let's get this revolution started!

*Another world is not only possible, she is on her way. On a quiet day, I can hear her breathing.*

*Arundahti Roy*

## Introduction

Compassion can be a mighty act of resistance. By developing it, you are, in a thousand ways, bending the arc towards justice. Throughout this book, you have learned about the ways that compassion grows and manifests itself in your life and in the lives of others. This final chapter is an invitation to generously create what Charles Eisenstein called, 'The more beautiful world our hearts know is possible.' This world will come about when we recognise that we are all interconnected, we belong to each other and we share a common humanity. If you are suffering, I am suffering. That is the basis of compassion. This is how we will make a compassionate world, we will roll up our sleeves, find our brave, and build something new.

The next iteration of the economic, social and political future is emerging and it is a bolder paradigm. Of that, I have no doubt.

As we extend our arms wide to midwife this new world into existence, there are three important themes that I am paying attention to and nurturing in my own work. This chapter offers each of these to you for your consideration.

1. How we build the future: The way we build the next wave of economic, social and political life will determine our future.
2. Healing the world: There is a pounding weight of trauma in the world that we have mostly ignored and allowed to grow unheeded. Compassion is the central fulcrum. Archimedes knew that with a fulcrum you can move the world.
3. Joy in the journey: One of the most beautiful lessons for me over the last two years has been discovering the joy in the work we do as Revolutionaries.

## How we build the future

> *What is at stake is a new world order in which people in all their full diversity, complexity and humanity share power over the decisions, resources and stories that shape their physical health and mental wellbeing.*
>
> *Jonathan Cohen*

The COVID-19 pandemic has given rise to much pro-social behaviour. All the social distancing and hand sanitising, wearing face masks, caring for our neighbours. There has been a rhetoric of 'we're all in this together'. But are we? Really?

The evidence tells us that the effects of COVID-19, far from being indiscriminate, follow deeply entrenched patterns of health inequities, mirroring burdens of disease that are near universal. People with resources, money, and power, often majority racial or ethnic groups, are better able to physically distance themselves by working from home, and outsourcing the work of keeping their pantry full to people on less pay who put their health at risk working in a supermarket or delivering food. Our health systems have structural violence and inequity baked into them.

Martin Luther King Jr spoke often of compassion, enjoining us to see that compassion ultimately motivates us not to '[fling] a coin to a beggar' but 'to see that the edifice which produces beggars needs restructuring'. Compassion pushes us to understand how we have structured the world, and to ask how we can re-structure it. Not only so we may suffer less, but because others are suffering, and their distress is ours.

We are in a transition from one epoch to another. Care-less to care. Mechanistic to human-centred.

We're living into the change we need right now, so we can create new ways of relating to each other and new ways of being in the world.

A friend of mine, Robert Wood, has recently taken to writing letters as a tool for change he wants to see in the world. Not the standard petitioning we have come to think of as letter writing as a campaign but a more gentle and poetic form of appeal to our common humanity. I delight in reading his letters and the replies.

Recently Robert wrote to his local pub to suggest that the name of the hotel might be out of step with our shared values of respect. The thing I love about the letter is that Robert doesn't lecture to the publican or make a claim about some truth. He assumes best intentions and writes with a generous compassion because in his words 'where we have a frothy and a chinwag matters.'

*March 17th 2021*
*Dear Rob and Karen*

*I trust all is well. My name is Robert Wood and I love your pub. I have had a relationship to this region since 1991 when my parents bought a place in Redgate. Over the years, I have moved around but always loved returning to this beautiful part of the world. Your pub has been integral to that, and there have been many gigs, pints and meals I have shared with family, friends and strangers over the years. Congratulations on running such a wonderful venue and successful business.*

*My letter has been a difficult one to write. There is no easy way to bring this up – but I feel like I have to. I have always referred to it as 'the Tav', which is its name to everyone in town. I love that name, but I also wonder if the official name of The Settlers is suited to the times.*

*As you would have seen across the media, and also in food stories, protests and other things at the moment there is a lot of contention about how we talk about our identity and our past. This extends to calls by many in the community for a truth telling and reconciliation process that helps to heal old wounds caused by invasion, colonisation, and, indeed, what we call settlers.*

*That brings me to the difficult part of my email. I find 'Settlers' to be a word that can have negative connotations, which matter in our part of the world, where there was a massacre just up the road in Metricup; and it can often mask what many people see as invasion. I know that you personally do not want to cause offence and I have always found the Tav to be a welcoming environment for all ages, all races, and all visitors. And yet, and yet, I wonder if the name 'Settlers' is outdated and could be misread? So, to my question, would you consider renaming the pub to simply be 'The Tav'?*

*People might say, this is political correctness gone mad, but I think it is an important step in our journey as a people to speak truthfully about what happens and to celebrate the good things here. I hope you don't find my question impolite, and the day you plant the seed is not the day you pick the fruit. So, take your time and consider what I have said. Thanks for listening.*

When I first read this letter and the subsequent response, my eyes welled with tears and I felt something inside me crack a little and open up. I am sure it was joy. The Tav wrote back thanking Robert for his beautiful letter and engaged wholeheartedly with the issues he had raised. They promised to think this over. I was all at once overcome by how we can so simply bend the moral arc towards justice. With our words, leaving our ego aside, we come alongside others, all the time knowing full well 'the day we plant the seed is not the day we pick the fruit'. I don't know when the name of the pub will change, or indeed if it will change but I feel certain that a seed was planted that will bear fruit.

The American social activist and essayist, Grace Lee Boggs, was heavily involved in the remaking of Detroit. Grace and her partner James Boggs, a political activist, created the Detroit Summer in the early 90s. This movement rebuilt Detroit and took what looked hopeless, dismal and burnt-out and created something new. Detroit stood as a symbol of the end of industrial society. Beautiful architectural marvels lay in ruins and entire neighborhoods lived behind bolted doors and barred windows.

Detroit Summer's activities included planting community gardens in vacant lots, creating huge murals on buildings and renovating houses. Most importantly this movement was centred on starting neighbourhood conversation projects and creating jobs and opportunities for people. In many ways the letter writing project that Robert has started is an example of a neighbourhood conversation.

Grace Lee Boggs understood that change happens in small revolutions, it happens in transitions.

One of her central and crucial teachings was that we need to own the system before we can believe we can change it. We need to look at what we have made so that we may know that we can dismantle it and make something new. This healthcare system; this legal system; this education system; this policing system – we made them. They didn't appear before us as a terrifying mirage.

Grace Lee Boggs died in 2015 aged 100 years. The year before she died, she wrote this:

> *People are aware that they cannot continue in the same old way but are immobilized because they cannot imagine an alternative. We need a vision that recognizes that we are at one of the great turning points in human history when the survival of our planet and the restoration of our humanity require a great sea change in our ecological, economic, political, and spiritual values.*[1]

She believed that it is by working together in small groups that positive social change can happen, not in large revolutions where one group of power simply changes position with another.

This is exactly what Greta Thunberg the student climate activist has done. This brave, outspoken young woman, 15 years old when she stepped into the spotlight, wearing two long skinny pigtails and a rain jacket, sitting outside the Houses of Parliament in Sweden, striking from school to bring attention to global warming. Greta is perhaps best known for her Climate Change School Strike where thousands of children all over the world went on strike from school to demonstrate the importance of acting against climate change.

Greta said, 'You are never too small to make change.'

When she addressed the United Nations Climate Change Conference, she said,

*We have not come here to beg the world leaders to care. You have ignored us in the past and you will ignore us again. We have run out of excuses and we are running out of time. We have come here to let you know that change is coming whether you like it or not.[2]*

Powerful words. We can do this. We can decide that we are the change-makers we have been waiting for. We can usher in a new epoch of care. A new way of being in the workplace and of relating to each other with compassion and love. A new way of caring for our climate.

If you could have a conversation with someone today about how you might make change happen at your place of work, how you would declare your intention to create systems of care, not systems of care-less, who would you talk to? Who would be your comrade in arms? How would you come alongside someone with generosity? Find someone this week and have a conversation about bringing compassion alive where you work. This is what it means to be a compassion revolutionary. Then, after the conversation, make a promise together to act on it.

*The only way to deal with an unfree world is to become so absolutely free that your very existence is an act of rebellion.*
*Albert Camus*

Some days I get the sense that I'm pedalling so hard to make things better and I'm not seeing any change at all. Do you ever feel like that? People often imagine that I never get disheartened, but I do, just like you.

When I feel disheartened, I have to remind myself that people laid the groundwork for all the change that happens and often they don't see the fruit of their work or they don't recognise that their work was instrumental. Everything we see happen that is positive, groundbreaking or was a landmark didn't start with us. Just because the work we do doesn't see any fruit doesn't make it any less important.

One of my favourite books is by Rebecca Solnit: *Hope in the Dark.* She talks about the way change happens incrementally and encourages us to stay hopeful –

> *After a rain, mushrooms appear on the surface of the earth as if from nowhere. Many of these mushrooms appear from a vast underground fungus that remains invisible and largely unknown. What we call mushrooms mycologists call the fruiting body of the larger, less visible fungus. It's like that with revolutions.*
>
> *Uprisings and revolutions are often considered to be spontaneous. They're not. There is always less visible long-term organizing and groundwork – or underground work – this work often laid the foundation.*
>
> *When we see changes in ideas and values we need to remember that these changes resulted from work done by writers, scholars, public intellectuals, social activists, and ordinary people with a hashtag.*[3]

I heard a story on a podcast (I can't even remember what podcast or when I heard it) from a woman who was an anti-nuclear weapons activist in the 70s. She saw herself as an ordinary middle-aged woman, standing on a street corner every week holding a sign – sometimes it was raining and sometimes it was hot. But she was diligent. Each week she met with others and together they held their placards. She often wondered if she was wasting her time. She would ask herself, 'Am I making any difference at all?' You know those moments when we say to ourselves 'should I give this game away?' I have moments like that.

Many, many years later the woman with the placard was listening to Dr Benjamin Spock on the radio. Dr Spock, for those of you who are old enough to remember, was an American paediatrician who wrote the book *Baby and Child Care* in the 1940s. It was one of the best-selling volumes on paediatric care in history. Most western children born in the 50s and 60s were parented according to Dr Spock's theories – some of which were actually quite enlightening.

He was also a prominent anti-nuclear weapons activist and his work in this area made a great impact on the trajectory of our world.

In the radio interview, Dr Spock was reflecting on his life and the interviewer asked him, 'What convinced you to step up and speak out so boldly against nuclear weapons?'

He said this: 'Well, one day I was walking through New York and I saw a woman, just an ordinary person standing in the rain, holding a placard, getting wet. But making her point known. And I thought to myself, if she can do that, in the rain, week in, week out, I can do it too. It gave me courage to step up.'

At that very moment the woman with the placard discovered that all those afternoons holding her placard in the rain had actually changed the course of history.

We don't know who is watching us. We don't know who is modelling themselves on our behaviour, who we encourage or who we discourage. And so we keep going.

# Healing the world

> *Later that night*
> *I held an atlas in my lap*
> *ran my fingers across the whole world*
> *and whispered*
> *where does it hurt?*
> *it answered*
> *everywhere*
> *everywhere*
> *everywhere.*
>
> *Warsan Shire*[4]

To bring healing and compassion to the world as we change it, we need an activism that doesn't demoralise but remoralises people. This is an activism where we don't dismiss or deride or take advantage of others.

So here's the warning right up front for all the revolutionaries: stay off the war path! Do not reproduce in our own activism the same oppressive mentalities that we seek to change and transform in the wider world. Don't use the 'master's tools', as Audre Lourde reminded us. They will not dismantle the master's house. Shaming, blaming, ridiculing, deriding, belittling, outsmarting, posturing and competing – these are the blunt instruments we are most used to in public debate. But this is what Tim Hiersted calls Compassionate Activism.[5]

> *Compassionate activism is an activism that is ready for the war to end. We're looking forward to the day we can put down all weapons, both physical and verbal, and embrace each other as the family that we truly are.*

Writer and sociologist John Holloway, author of *Crack Capitalism*, argued that the way to achieve what's needed is to create cracks in capitalist domination spaces or moments in which we live out our dream of being truly human. I think of these created spaces as small everyday acts of resistance that shape the way the world moves and the way we stand with each other to defy the rule to care less in favour of caring more.

In 2018, I visited Berlin and I spent some time at the Topography of Terror, the museum on the site that once housed the most important institutions of Nazi terror – the National Headquarters of the Secret State Police (Gestapo) and the Reich SS Leadership. I was walking on the same stone floors that members of Hitler's entourage walked on.

In 1933, there was this widespread feeling of liberation across Germany. People no longer wanted democracy. They wanted this strong, popular leader. That's how Hitler came to be in power, essentially. This is eerily similar to the popularist obsession we have in politics today. At the Topography of Terror, I came across a collection of old, grainy, black and white photographs of workers at the Blohm+Voss Shipyards. These were just ordinary men and women. One of the photos was taken during the singing of the national anthem following the Führer's address. Everyone in the photo had raised their right arm. It was that obligatory German salute. But when I looked closely at the photograph, there was one man who sat quietly with his arms folded – a bold move with the Führer in the room. Historians believe that this man was most likely named August Landmesser. He was no one extraordinary. He was just one man, not conforming and not following, risking everything to stay true to himself and to others.

Standing in front of his photo, I began to wonder how I could do more of that. I asked myself at that moment, 'what is one small act of resistance that I can perpetrate each day to stay true to myself?'

How do we transact kindness and love? How can we refuse to let it slip away? Maybe today is the perfect day to ask someone how they are, to touch someone's arm as you speak (COVID permitting) or to speak up and say, 'I belong to myself.'

Maybe you'll leave that styrofoam packing at the cash register, refuse the plastic straw, ask your colleague their preferred pronouns as you share yours or learn the names the traditional owners gave the lands you walk on. All the ways we can be like August Landmesser present themselves to us, every day, like tiny invitations. Invitations to act with respect and dignity. Invitations to share a moment of joy. Invitation to decolonise our language and our actions. If we can begin to see these little invitations as delightful steps in a dance we are clumsily learning, it will lighten the burden of our response. I don't have to get it right or perfect, I simply have to move to the beat of a new drum.

Sensing and intuiting the future requires us to be present with ourselves. In earlier chapters, you learned how to extend compassion towards yourself and others from that place of Showing Up. It is from this place that you will know the way to move through the world – with all its hallways winding endlessly through hospitals, under bridges where the tired and hungry sleep, in the cars of gig economy workers, carrying hot pizzas to your doors, and past the locked dementia wards where our parents may see out their days. It's in all these places that the future emerges, and your work is to usher it in.

Gregory C. Ellison founded Fearless Dialogues, a new movement for justice. He learned from his grandmother and aunt that you can't change the world, but he would say, 'You can change three feet in front of you.' With metric conversion, that's one metre around you. This practice will see us take responsibility for making change in our personal proximity as a daily habit. Maybe we could carry a tape measure with us daily as a reminder that we can take responsibility for influencing that part of the world that we occupy.

## Joy in the work

> *It seems simple – but people stay more engaged in a space*
> *where they are enjoying each other, and feel celebrated and*
> *appreciated. Small personal celebrations help fuel groups*
> *through the hard work, reminding them that they are*
> *humans together, regardless of the external pressures they face.*
> *adrienne maree brown*[6]

One of the most beautiful lessons has been discovering the joy in the work we do as revolutionaries, changing the world. People often ask me how I remain so optimistic and hopeful. I am hopeful because I am not so arrogant as to think that I know what will happen next. I am happy because, as Audre Lorde said, 'I am who I am, doing what I came to do'. The world will always ask something of us and we will have our own demands of the world; things we want and things we are striving to achieve. The joy rises up when these two circles overlap. I try and live in the small space where the world and I agree. Where the universe and I want the same thing for me. It's a bit like living on a tightrope, but thankfully love is the balancing pole that keeps me stepping out one foot in front of the other. This is where the joy is for all of us.

There is a compounding weight of trauma in the world that we have mostly ignored and allowed to grow unheeded. Compassion is the central fulcrum. Archimedes knew that with a fulcrum, you can move the world.

Our work must be seated in an experience of joy that we bring to the work and extract from it. The Industrial Revolution dismembered joy from the body of our work and our job is to bring it back to the centre.

In 2017, the Institute for Healthcare Improvement in Boston released the Framework for Improving Joy in Work.[7] I happened to be visiting the Institute at the time that they were working on this framework, so I've always been keenly interested to see the final product. In 2019, the American Medical Association launched the Joy in Medicine program.[8] Both of these pieces of work are about creating and recognising organisations that demonstrate efforts to improve clinician satisfaction and reduce burnout – one by providing an award and the other by providing a template for how we might increase joy in our workplace.

Healthcare industries have recognised that joy is a currency, and it's one that they're banking on to buy them out of increasing burnout. But real joy is a sign of resilience and wellbeing. It's deep-seated and it's about us doing what we were born to do. When I work with organisations, I don't have to drill very far to find that the wellspring of joy has been dammed up, converted into a five step 'easy to remember' set of values that no one can remember or has been outsourced to the two enthusiastic and overworked clinicians who are fast burning out. I rarely see a budget for joy or a cost centre for compassion.

There's an overwhelming 1950s view of what life at work should be like and it's based on a number of erroneous premises. One is that we never bring our pain to the workplace, and the other is that work is serious business. In all my visits to places where people work – organisations, small teams, large teams – I always try to bring with me this sense of joy and happiness. I find that where people are connected to the happiness of their work or the true reason that they went into this work in the first place, there is a sense of wanting to contribute to the wellbeing of the world. As I help people to reach in and own that again, it releases the energy and enthusiasm that we need to do even difficult work. Work isn't all about serious business, particularly if you're working in healthcare. Work is about connecting with other human beings and delighting in both their strength and fragility as we lead them into a place where they begin to become more well or learn to manage their illness with more ease.

You may be asking me right this moment inside your head, 'How can I be joyful when the system is in chaos and it's crumbling before my eyes?' Many of our systems right now are crumbling. But they're inhabited by human beings. The beauty and the joy is always present for us and can be seen in a multitude of ways. Don't let the artefacts of your organisation – its rules, policies, procedures and demands – blind you to the beauty of being able to connect with humans.

Lack of joy isn't a deficit. It's a symptom that things are out of balance and there needs to be collective effort for correction. Don't take your lack of joy as a fait accompli, see it as a symptom for change.

Let joy be your barometer. When there are times in your life where you feel there is simply no joy left in the work that you are doing, step back from that, come back into this present moment and follow the steps of SUMA.

1. Show up
2. Understand
3. Move Closer
4. Act.

This simple decision will help you reconnect with the joy that is available for you. Each step can be light. That doesn't mean that everything is laugh a minute, it just means that there is a powerful sense of purpose that arises in the work that you do and in who you are. You are a cause for happiness in the lives of others. Even if you never achieved another thing. Someone, somewhere would feel their heart full just thinking about you.

The world doesn't necessarily want you to be joyful, but as a tiny little act of resistance, you can let a river of joy flow.

## Conclusion

The future is coming, and you and I are responsible for shaping it. You are at a point, right now, where you can take everything that you have gathered throughout the reading of this book and step right into the present shining moment.

When I was in Boston in 2016, it was graduation day at Harvard and the speaker was actress Rashida Jones. She looked down into the crowd and said:

> *When big decisions pop up, get quiet, real quiet. Turn off your phone, turn off your computer, and listen to your true heart. And hear the thing that makes you feel sick with excitement, that scares you because you know you'll learn and do that thing.*

This is my wholehearted advice to you, dear reader. The world is changing and you – more than anyone else – deserve love, joy and compassion.

You are the change I have been waiting for.

# Conclusion

You were born with the innate biological and neurophysiological capacity for compassion. It is your birthright, and every day you are invited to extend this essential goodness towards yourself and others. Along the way, we have all drifted far from a solid belief that we are deserving of our own care and compassion. We have all found ways to push ourselves to the point of exhaustion and to distract ourselves from the present moment. We have internalised the voice of capitalism that urges us to work until exhaustion, strive for power and achievement and fill our homes with more stuff. We have collectively created systems of care that value throughput and measure success in the number of 'bed days' or time spent waiting for service. Throughout this book, you have discovered that compassion is the force that will mend the world, starting with a space just in front of you.

I can't promise you that after reading this book your hair will shine and your cheeks will glow, although you may very well get that result as a byproduct of being exactly who you were born to be – a Compassion Revolutionary. But what will happen is that you will fall in love a little more, with yourself and those around you. You'll notice that the distance between you and others begins to shorten, and one day you will wake up knowing deep in your heart that we are all connected through our common humanity. You will see clearly, maybe for the very first time, that everyone is carrying their own trauma, fear and insecurity – just like you. Everyone is looking for love and connection. This knowledge will be your nourishment and your joy.

As you wake each morning, say hello to wherever you are and greet the day with open-heartedness. Show up big for yourself and others. Seek to understand with simple clarity what will bring more compassion into the situation. Move closer to the distress that you see before you. Act with good intentions. Touch your heart softly and come home to yourself, the place where you belong. These are the four steps of SUMA that you will practise lightly, knowing that every moment is a new beginning.

Change will come about as we move closer to the power of compassionate action. It will start in small ways, through tiny acts of resistance. We will practise the many small ways that we can resist what is expected of us – when we hold the door open for someone; when we ask people how they are and wait for the answer; when we tenderly touch someone's arm; and when we offer cool water. All these things are ways that we bring compassion alive. Once you understand the cumulative power of your actions, you can change the part of the world that you occupy, even if it's only that one metre in front of you.

You are a Compassion Revolutionary. You step forward, knowing that you are not alone as you bend the arc towards justice. Every moment is a new opportunity to start again, just like each breath is a new opportunity to fill our lungs with oxygen. Each moment of rest is a chance to be refreshed.

As you come to the end of this book you may be feeling overwhelmed by the task ahead. I chose the term 'revolution' purposefully and carefully because I believe that it's in these small groups where we start to make feasible and scalable change that will happen in that one metre in front of us. Don't be overwhelmed. You were born to connect with others and you were born as a compassionate and loving human being. This is your birthright. Standing with yourself is a powerful mechanism that has been used historically throughout every time of great change and it continues to work for us today at the grocery store. We belong to ourselves. We have agency and power to make decisions, however small they are.

You may feel inertia, fear, panic, self-consciousness and the crushing weight of distraction. Remember, the very first step is showing up. Showing up is where we come into this present moment, not believing that the next moment is more exciting or more important. Put your feet on the ground and press our heels down and feel the support of the earth.

As we build the future, I encourage you to find joy in the journey – joy that builds you up and unleashes your bravery and energy.

My prayer for you, dear Compassion Revolutionary –

> *May you find the courage to start right now and hold a clear*
> *and shining hope for the future you are making. May your*
> *heart be filled with joy and lightness as you stay the path.*
> *May you keep going.*

# Connect with me

I'm reminded of the poet Mary Oliver, who wrote *Instructions for Living A Life*.

> *Pay attention.*
> *Be astonished.*
> *Tell someone about it.*

This is my invitation to you, dear reader. As you begin to notice compassion in action, share the news.

Join me at **compassionrevolution.care** and bring others.

Use the hashtag #compassionrevolution on socials.

Let's find each other, and celebrate the audacity and delight of bringing the world alight with compassion at every step.

You've got this. Keep going.

Mary

# Acknowledgements

I want to acknowledge the enormous learning and transformation I have found in the writings of:

Tara Brach, adrienne maree brown, Tarana Burke, Pema Chödrön, Augustín Fuentes, Roxanne Gay, Ross Gay, Amanda Gorman, Ibram X kendi, Robin Wall Kimmerer, Jaqueline Novagratz, Resmaa Menakem, Kae Tempest, Pádraig Ó Tuama, Lama Rod Owens, Layla Saad, Sharon Salzberg, Rebecca Solnit, Brother David Steindl-Rast OSB, Sonya Renee Taylor, David Whyte.

During the writing of this book, I discovered the music of Abigail and Shaun Bengson (The Bengsons) and their *Keep Going* song and later *My Joy is Heavy* and *Hope Comes* sustained me.

Thank you to Kath Walters, my Book Coach, who kept my eyes on the prize: publication. My Editor Karen Comer, your insight was a gift to me.

Over the course of writing this book I went on a series of Writing Retreats with my dearest friend Lia. I cannot thank you enough for reminding me that writing a book is a process of sitting with discomfort and doing hard work to bring big ideas to life. Your expertise was a light on my path and your encouragement was everything.

My dearest ones: Geoff, Jessie, Chelsea and Audrey. You are my world.

I owe a deep gratitude to those who supported me to keep going. Thank you to my friends Kirsty, Michael and Pete for being all the things. My sisters, Margie and Zeta, for your love and encouragement.

My first readers Shannon Weber and Jane Munro. These women took my messy first draft and held it with love and respect and returned it to me with instructions for how to make it the book you are holding right now.

# Notes

**Introduction**

1. You can read all about the Compassion Labs at www.compassionrevolution.care

2. Boggs, G. L., et al, *The next American revolution: Sustainable activism for the twenty-first century*, University of California Press, 2012.

3. Cohen, J. 'A Time for Optimism? Decolonizing the Determinants of Health', *Journal of Health and Human Rights*, 2020, https://www.hhrjournal.org/2020/11/a-time-for-optimism-decolonizing-the-determinants-of-health/

4. Büyüm, A. M., Kenney. C., Koris, A., et al, 'Decolonising global health: if not now, when?' *BMJ Global Health,* 2020, https://gh.bmj.com/content/bmjgh/5/8/e003394.full.pdf

5. These ideas are illuminated at https://www.fhi360.org/

**Chapter One – Compassion is not a special project**

1. Kelley, J. M., Kraft-Todd, G., Schapira, L., Kossowsky, J., & Riess, H., 'The influence of the patient-clinician relationship on healthcare outcomes: a systematic review and meta-analysis of randomized controlled trials', *Plos one*, 9 (4), 2014.

2. Functional magnetic resonance imaging (fMRI) measures the small changes in blood flow that occur with brain activity.

3.   Lunsted, H., Smith, T., Layton, B., 'Social relationships and mortality risk: A meta-analytic review', *Plos,* 2010, https://doi.org/10.1371/journal.pmed.1000316

4.   Klimecki, O. M., Leiberg, S., Lamm, C., & Singer, T., 'Functional neural plasticity and associated changes in positive affect after compassion training', *Cerebral cortex* (New York), 23 (7), pp. 1552–1561, 2013. https://doi.org/10.1093/cercor/bhs142

5.   Pearson, C. M., and Porath, C. L., *The cost of bad* behavior: *how incivility is damaging your business and what you can do about it,* New York, Portfolio Hardcover, 2009.

6.   Perry, B., and Winfrey, O., *What Happened To You?* New York: Flatiron Books, 2021.

7.   Westbrook, J., Sunderland, N., Li, L., Koyama, A., McMullan, R., Urwin, R., Churruca, K., Baysari, M. T., Jones, C., Loh, E., McInnes, E. C., Middleton, S., & Braithwaite, J. 'The prevalence and impact of unprofessional behaviour among hospital workers: a survey in seven Australian hospitals', *The Medical journal of Australia,* 214 (1), pp. 31–37, 2021. https://doi.org/10.5694/mja2.50849

8.   Riskin, A., Erez, A., Foulk, T. A., Kugelman, A., Gover, A., Shoris, I., Riskin, K. S., & Bamberger, P. A., 'The impact of rudeness on medical team performance: A randomized trial', *Pediatrics,* 136 (3), pp. 487–495, 2015. https://doi.org/10.1542/peds.2015-1385

9.   Egbert, L. D., Battit G. E., Welch, C. E., and Bartlett, M. K., 'Reduction of post-operative pain by encouragement and instruction of patients: A study of doctor patient rapport', *The New England journal of medicine,* 270, pp. 825–827, 1964. https://doi.org/10.1056/NEJM196404162701606

10.  Redelmeier, D. A., Molin, J. P., & Tibshirani, R. J., 'A randomised trial of compassionate care for the homeless in an emergency department', *Lancet,* 345 (8958), pp. 1131–1134. https://doi.org/10.1016/s0140-6736(95)90975-3

11.  Torpie, K., *Losing face: A memoir of lost identity and Self discovery,* New Zealand: Harper Collins, 2005.

12.  Porath, C., 'No time to be nice at work', *New York Times,* 19 June, 2015. https://www.nytimes.com/2015/06/21/opinion/sunday/is-your-boss-mean.html

**Chapter Two – What is compassion?**

1.  Gilbert. P., Choden. K., (2014). *Mindful compassion: How the science of compassion can help you understand your emotions, live in the present and connect more deeply with others*, New Harbinger Publications, 2014.
2.  Sweeney. K., 'Mesothelioma', *BMJ*, 2009. https://www.bmj.com/content/339/bmj.b2862/rapid-responses
3.  Bloom, P., *Against empathy: The case for rational compassion*, Harper Collins, New York, 2016.
4.  Ibid.
5.  Bradt, S., 'Wandering mind not a happy mind', *Harvard Gazette*, 2019. https://news.harvard.edu/gazette/story/2010/11/wandering-mind-not-a-happy-mind/
6.  I was inspired to create this practice after reading Padraig O'Tuoma's book, *In the shelter: Finding a home in the world*.
7.  O'Tuoma, Padraig, *In the shelter: Finding a home in the world*, John Murray, 2016.
8.  Chödrön, P., *When things fall apart: Heart advice* for *difficult times*, Boston: Shambala, 2000. I bought this book when it was first published and I have never really stopped reading it.
9.  Weber, S., *Show up hard: A roadmap for helpers in crisis*, 2018.
10. https://www.dictionaryofobscuresorrows.com/post/235369 22667/sonder
11. Worline. M., and Dutton. J., *Awakening compassion at work: the quiet power that elevates people and organizations*, NY: McGraw-Hill Education, 2017.
12. Chödrön, P., *When things fall apart: Heart advice for difficult times*, Boston: Shambala, 2000.
13. I use the Insight Timer App.

**Chapter Three – The science of compassion**

1.  Leibermann, M., *Social: Why our brains* are *wired to connect*, New York: Crown Publishers, 2014.
2.  Ibid.
3.  Halifax J., *Standing at the edge: Finding freedom where fear and courage meet*, New York: Flatiron Books, 2018.
4.  Kerr, F., and Maze, L., 'The art and science of looking up', 2019. https://www.lookup.org.au/report

5.   de Waal, F. B. M., *Our inner ape: A leading primatologist explains why we are who we are*, New York: Riverhead Books, 2005.

6.   White Body Supremacy is the term preferred by Resmaa Menakem. Refer to his book *My Grandmother's Hands: Racialized Trauma and the Pathways to Mending Our Hearts and Bodies*, Central Recovery Press.

7.   DiAngelo, R., *What does it mean to be white? Developing white racial literacy*, New York: Peter Lang, 2016.

8.   Kyle 'Guante' Tran Myhre. https://guante.info/2020/11/22/nottheshark/

9.   Code Grey is an emergency response to situations/incidents of verbal and/or physical aggression, threatening behaviour, abuse and violence involving patients, visitors, relatives, VMOs or caregivers.

10.  In 2021, Dr Miriam-Rose Ungunmerr-Baumann was honoured as the Senior Australian of the Year. It is recognition for a lifetime of work as a teacher and role model in her Daly River (Nauiyu) community. In 1975, Miriam-Rose became the Northern Territory's first fully qualified Aboriginal teacher and a strong advocate for integrating art into mainstream education.

11.  Dr Miriam Rose – I highly recommend watching this entrancing video about Dadirri https://www.youtube.com/watch?v=tow2tR_ezL8

12.  Emma Seppälä teaches at Yale School of Management and the Stanford Centre for Compassion and Altruism Research and Education.

13.  Philippot, P., Chapelle, G. and Blairy, S., (2002) Respiratory feedback in the generation of emotion, *Cognition and Emotion*, 16:5, 605-627, DOI: 10.1080/02699930143000392

**Chapter Four – Self-compassion**

1.   Self-Compassion.org. https://self-compassion.org/

2.   Ibid.

3.   I recommend checking out The Bengsons (Abigail and Shaun) on Spotify.

4.   Visit Shannon Weber's LoveYou2 website for Love Note templates https://www.loveyou2.org/.

**Chapter Five – Compassion for others**

1.  Lameris, D., "Poem: Small Kindnesses", *New York Times*, September 19, 2019, https://www.nytimes.com/2019/09/19/magazine/poem-small-kindnesses.html

2.  Halifax., J., *Standing at the edge: Finding freedom where fear and courage meet*, New York: Flatiron Books, 2018.

3.  Merton, T., *Conjectures of a guilty bystander*, Garden City, NY: Doubleday, 1966.

4.  Solnit, R., *Hope in the dark: untold histories, wild possibilities*, New York: Nation Books, 2004.

5.  Tippett, K., *On Being*, 18 February, 2021, Ariel Burger: Be a blessing. [audio podcast] retrieved from https://onbeing.org/programs/ariel-burger-be-a-blessing/

6.  Ibid.

7.  http://compassionrevolution.care

8.  Eamons, R. and McCullogh, M., 'Counting blessings versus burdens', *Journal of Personality and Social Psychology*, Vol. 84, No. 2, pp. 377–389, 2003.

**Chapter Six – Taking compassion to work**

1.  https://www.smh.com.au/national/nsw/westmead-hospital-icu-stripped-of-training-accreditation-over-alleged-bullying-20181026-p50c8j.html

2.  'Damning AMA survey reveals the toll of overworking junior doctors', *Sydney Morning Herald*, 6 June, 2017, https://www.smh.com.au/healthcare/damning-ama-survey-reveals-the-toll-of-overworking-junior-doctors-20170606-gwlbdv.html.

3.  https://www.smh.com.au/national/treament-ills-as-doctors-battle-depression-20140925-10lupw.html

4.  Humans of NY Facebook page https://www.facebook.com/humansofnewyork/posts/1253024261438338:0

5.  Xu, T., Magnusson-Hanson, L., et al., 'Workplace bullying and workplace violence as risk factors for cardiovascular disease: a multi-cohort study', *European Heart Journal*, Vol 40, Issue 14, 2019. https://doi.org/10.1093/eurheartj/ehy683

6.  Shanafelt, T. D., Balch, C. M., Dyrbye, L., Bechamps, G., Russell, T., Satele, D., Rummans, T., Swartz, K., Novotny, P. J., Sloan, J.,

& Oreskovich, M. R., 'Special report: suicidal ideation among American surgeons', *Archives of surgery* (1960), 146 (1), pp. 54–62, 2011. https://doi.org/10.1001/archsurg.2010.292

7. Bartram, D., and Baldwin. D., 'Veterinary surgeons and suicide: influences, opportunities and research directions', *Vet Rec* 162: 36-40, 2008.

8. Pei, K., and Cochran, A., 'Workplace bullying among surgeons: The perfect crime', *Annals of Surgery*, 2019. Volume 269, Issue 1, p 43–44

9. 'Long working hours: increasing deaths from heart attack and stroke', WHO and ILO, 17 May 2021, Joint News Release: Geneva, 2021.

10. Zaslow. J., 'New index aims to calculate the annual cost of despair', WSJ. 20 Nov. 2002. https://www.wsj.com/articles/ SB103773937895627388.

11. Boggs, G. L., 'Reimagine Everything', *Reimagine*, Vol. 19, No. 2, 2021. https://www.reimaginerpe.org/19-2/boggs

12. Ibid.

13. Singh, J., 'How Jacinda Ardern sets a new global benchmark for leadership', *The Frontier Post*, 2019. https://thefrontierpost.com/ how-jacinda-ardern-sets-a-new-global-benchmark-for-leadership-%E2%80%8B/

14. Ardern, J., 'Jacinda Ardern on the Christchurch shooting', *The Guardian*, 15 March 2019. https://www.theguardian.com/ world/2019/mar/15/one-of-new-zealands-darkest-days-jacinda-ardern-responds-to-christchurch-shooting

15. Worline, M., and Dutton.,J., *Awakening compassion at work: the quiet power that elevates people and organizations*, NY: McGraw-Hill Education, 2017.

16. West, M., Collins, B., Eckert, R., Chowla, R., *Caring to change: How compassionate leadership can stimulate innovation in health care*, London: Kings Fund, 2017. https://www.kingsfund.org.uk/ publications/caring-change

17. West, M., and Dawson, J., *Employee engagement and NHS performance*, London: Kings Fund, 2012. https://www.kingsfund. org.uk/sites/default/files/employee-engagement-nhs-performance-west-dawson-leadership-review2012-paper.pdf

18. West., M., and Dawson, J., 'NHS Staff Management and Health Service Quality', Lancaster University Management School and The Work Foundation Aston Business School, (undated). https://assets. publishing.service.gov.uk/government/uploads/system/uploads/ attachment_data/file/215454/dh_129658.pdf

19. You can discover more about Compassion Collaboratives at https://compassionrevolution.care/compassion-initiatives

**Chapter Seven – Let's get this revolution started!**

1. Boggs, G. L., https://charterforcompassion.org/truth-political-and-social-activists/truth-grace-lee-boggs

2. Mesey, C., 'Greta Thunberg's speech to the world', *Geneva Business News*, 21 December, 2018. https://www.gbnews.ch/greta-thunbergs-speech-to-the-world/

3. Solnit, R, *Hope in the dark: untold histories, wild possibilities*, New York: Nation Books, 2004.

4. https://www.poetryfoundation.org/poets/warsan-shire

5. Hjersted. T., *The compassionate activist toolkit: The ultimate guide to love centred activism,* Films For Action, 2016. https://www. filmsforaction.org/articles/the-compassionate-activist-toolkit/

6. brown, a. m., *Holding change: The way of emergent strategy, facilitation and mediation*, Edinburgh: A.K. Press, 2021.

7. Perlo, J., Balik, B., Swensen, S., Kabcenell, A., Landsman, J., Feeley, D., *IHI Framework for Improving Joy in Work*, IHI White Paper, Cambridge, Massachusetts: Institute for Healthcare Improvement, 2017.

8. American Medical Association, 'Joy in Medicine: Health System recognition Program', 2021. https://www.ama-assn.org/system/ files/2020-10/joy-award-brochure.pdf.